INSULTS AND PUNS
FOR LOVE AND MARRIAGE

Also by Louis A. Safian
2000 INSULTS FOR ALL OCCASIONS
JUST FOR THE PUN OF IT

LOUIS A. SAFIAN

INSULTS AND PUNS
FOR LOVE AND MARRIAGE

CITADEL PRESS · *Secaucus, New Jersey*

Copyright © 1966 by Louis A. Safian
All rights reserved
Published by Citadel Press
A division of Lyle Stuart Inc.
120 Enterprise Ave., Secaucus, N.J. 07094
In Canada: Musson Book Company
A division of General Publishing Co. Limited
Don Mills, Ontario
Manufactured in the United States of America
ISBN 0-8065-0851-5

Originally published as:
An Irreverent Dictionary of Love and Marriage

TO MY WIFE REA
who puts a grain of sugar into everything she says to me and takes everything I say with a grain of salt

CONTENTS

Introduction · 9

PART ONE
A Potpourri of Definitions Pertaining to Love and Marriage · 15

PART TWO

1 Love · 87
 Definitions 87
 At Love's Quipping Post 94

2 Marriage · 99
 Definitions 99
 Kinds of Marriage 108
 At the Matrimonial Quipping Post 110
 Storm Warnings 118

3 Husbands vs. Wives · 121
 Definitions 121
 Familiar Types 126
 Wives (of a Sort) 128
 The Trouble with Wives 137
 Storm Warnings 144
 The Widows They Leave Behind 146

4 Wives vs. Husbands 148
  Definitions 148
  Familiar Types 151
  Husbands (of a Sort) 153
  The Wife's Merry-Go-Round 157
  Storm Warnings 163

5 Divorce 165
  Definitions 165
  Adieu 169

6 Odds and Ends 173

7 Epitaphs for Departed Spouses 185

INTRODUCTION

No one can deny that cynical and comic definitions are popular branches of trenchant humor. More and more newspapers, magazines, trade journals, and house organs use them regularly as fillers for the amusement of their readers under such captions as Chuckles, Laffinitions, Deft-initions, and Daffynitions.

There are few experiences in life that escape the comic lexicographer's pen. But the situations created by love, marriage, and divorce are by far his most frequent sources of irreverent quips, satirical banter, spiced comments, and salty observations.

For the cynic, these topics are grist to his mill of barbed definitions of the many-faceted problems that confront the sexes in their daily lives. As one who is said to look both ways before crossing a one-way street, and who thinks the world never changes but only shortchanges, his comments on love and marriage run their critical route from mockery to verbal mayhem.

Although plentifully filled with the acerbic wit and acid-etched shafts of cynics, misanthropes, misogynists, snipers, and saboteurs of love and marriage, this volume has essentially been designed as the largest compilation of humorous and sportive definitions in connection exclusively with these topics ever, to my knowledge, to be found in one volume in dictionary form.

With a hearty laugh at our human failings, we can definitely add something worth while to our philosophy of living. An ancient sage once said: "Humor is the test of gravity, and gravity of humor; for the subject which will not bear raillery is suspicious, and the jest which will not bear serious examination is certainly false wit." Thus the wits, refusing to take seriously the sentimentalist's romantic notion of love and marriage as states of heavenly bliss, have spun a waggish web of definitions and epigrams around both conditions which, despite their elements of exaggeration, caricature, nonsense, and flippancy, are nonetheless edged with the sharp blades of realism and truth.

If many of these brash and acrimonious definitions and aphorisms appear to disfavor the female of the species, the distaff side can always find solace in the witticism that the trouble with most women is most men, and that if—as the presuming male claims—women are humorless, it is because God made women without a sense of humor so they could love their husbands instead of laughing at them.

It is hoped that this book will achieve its three primary objectives: first, to present the reader with an entertaining, diverting, and titillating collection of definitions and pungent sayings concerning love and marriage; second, to provide a

Introduction

handy source of humorous material for anyone who has occasion to comment on these topics in speeches or writings; last, but not least, to serve as a guidepost that may lead the reader to a broader insight and understanding in connection with the battle of the sexes.

I now entrust this volume to you, dear reader, with the thought that *marriage is both a loving and a laughing matter.*

Louis A. Safian

PART ONE

A

ADVICE

Information for which lawyers and psychiatrists charge fees, but which is given away free by your mother-in-law.

ALIMONY

The take from a mistake.

A contraction of the phrase "all his money."

A word often spelled "ali-moan-y" by divorced husbands.

The billing without the cooing.

A form of maintenance by which, if you don't pay in due time, you'll do time.

The high cost of loving.

The high cost of leaving.

Bounty on the mutiny.

Giving comfort to the enemy.

A time balm.

The matrimonial institution's severance pay.

A husband's cash-surrender value.

A pay-as-you-go plan.

Taxation without representation.

An allowance which enables a woman who was unhappily married to be happily unmarried.

A matter of wife and debt.

Heart-earned money.

A man's transition from a co-starring spot to a supporting role.

A pension that helps take the drudgery out of household duties.

The payment by one for the mistakes of two.

A *Potpourri of Definitions*

A war debt.

A wife's guaranteed annual wage.

The fee a woman charges for name-dropping.

A pay-as-you-burn plan.

A system like having the TV set on after one has fallen asleep.

Like buying oats for a dead horse.

Paying installments on a car after the wreck.

An award in court, where a woman says to her divorced husband, "'Bye now—pay later."

Matrimony's price of peace.

ANNIVERSARY

The day on which you forgot to buy your wife a present.

ANTIFREEZE

Your wife's new fur coat.

APOLOGY

The best way for a husband to get the last word.

ARGUMENT

Something a smart husband avoids. He might win; then he'd really be in trouble.

B

BABY-SITTER

A girl you hire to watch your television set.

Someone who, if memory serves, was once the baby's mother.

BACHELOR

A man who doesn't approve of marriage. He prefers to remain single and raise his children the same way.

What a man is called until he gets married—then you should hear what he calls himself.

A man who sees no sense in losing his best friend by marrying her.

One who believes everyone should be in love—which is exactly the reason one should never marry.

A chap who has taken out many a woman, but never been taken in.

A rolling stone that gathers no boss.

One who knows there are two kinds of men—the quick and the wed.

A man who believes in the survival of the fleetest.

A man who would rather be laughed at for not being married than not being able to laugh because he is.

A fellow who can come to his office each morning from a different direction.

One who believes it's better to have loved and lost—indeed, lots better.

A gay dog who cannot be spousebroken.

A man of un-altar-able views.

A man who can only be miss-led so far.

One who knows that none but the brave deserve the fair, but who's still glad he's a coward.

A Potpourri of Definitions

A fellow who steers clear of women with bride ideas.

One whose only objection to love is that it may become parsonfied.

A man who believes that even once in a wifetime is too much.

A man who has never met a woman he couldn't live without.

One who believes that being matrimonial-minded is a condition of the mind when the mind is out of condition.

One who nips in the bud a budding romance when he thinks of the blooming expense.

A man whose reflections say No when his reflexes say Yes.

One who may lean toward a woman but never enough to altar his stance.

One who doesn't subscribe to the idea that clever men make the best husbands. His idea is that clever men don't become husbands.

A man who won't play Troth or Consequences.

One who agrees that marriage is an institution and that marriage is love; but believes that since love is blind, marriage is an institution for the blind.

A man who adores women but never lets the feeling become nuptial.

One who believes that all wives dress to kill—and cook the same way.

A man who, in the land of the free and the home of the brave, would rather be free than brave.

One who avoids tying a knot around a woman's finger for fear of ending up under her thumb.

BACHELOR *(Continued)*

A fellow who likes his girl friend just the way she is—single.

A man who won't take a wife to share his life because he knows that shareholders often become directors.

A man who wants just one single thing in life—himself.

One who is keenly aware of the saying "Behind every man there's a woman"—and he doesn't intend to be caught.

A chap who doesn't intend to get billed for the time he cooed.

One who believes that what God has put asunder, no man shall join together.

A man who never has to worry how much of his take-home pay reaches there.

A man who regards marriage as like a girdle—easier to get into than to wriggle out of.

One who, when he walks the floor at midnight with a baby, is really dancing with her in a nightclub.

A man who sees no point in buying the cow when milk is so cheap.

A man who believes that love may be a sweet dream, but marriage is the alarm clock.

One who firmly believes in the guarantee of life, liberty, and the happiness of pursuit.

A happy-go-luck chap who can be seen anywhere with a woman except at the altar.

A man who when he speaks of "tying one on" doesn't mean an apron.

A *Potpourri of Definitions*

A man who hasn't let a woman pin anything on him since he was a baby.

One whose wallet is full of pictures of near-Mrs.

An obstinate grammarian. When asked to conjugate, he declines.

A fellow of double-talk and single purpose.

One who agrees that women may be a dime a dozen, but that when you cut that number down to one, it starts costing.

A chap who would rather be on the outside looking in than on the inside looking out.

A man who makes mistakes, but never in front of a preacher.

A happy-go-lucky individual who believes in wine, women, and so-long.

One who knows more about women than husbands do—or he'd be married too.

A man who looks before he lips.

An agile individual, who always has an arrow escape from Cupid.

BACHELOR PARTY

Where the prospective bridegroom has the kind of wonderful time he could have every night if he weren't getting married.

BANKRUPTCY

Insolvency; frequently due to a lack and a lass.

BARGAIN

Something your wife cannot use, at a price she cannot resist.

BATTLE OF THE SEXES

A war. which neither side can ever win—there's too much consorting with the enemy.

BEAUTY PARLOR

The place to which your wife is driven by the cosmetic urge.

BEST MAN

The one who isn't getting married.

The chap at the wedding who doesn't get a chance to prove it.

BETTER HALF

So called because if the wife wants something, her husband better have it.

BIGAMIST

A man who makes the same mistake twice.

A man who loves not wisely but two well.

A man who has married an attractive woman and a good cook.

A man who doesn't know when he's got enough.

A person who has taken one too many.

An individualist who wants to keep two himself.

A bored husband who decided to break the monogamy.

A man who has never heard of the proverb "No man can serve two masters."

A hogamist.

A *Potpourri of Definitions*

One who sees no crime in having one wife too many, when the very same thing may be said about monogamy.

One who believes that variety is the spice of wife.

BIGAMY

A crime for which the heaviest penalty is two mothers-in-law.

A criminal offense for which a good defense is a plea of insanity.

The only case on record where two rites make a wrong.

BIRD IMITATOR

A woman who watches her husband like a hawk.

BIRTH CONTROL

Evasion of the issue.

BIRTHDAY

The anniversary when the husband takes a day off and the wife a year off.

BLESSED EVENT

When a mother-in-law says she's going home.

BOOZER

A man who expects his wife to stick to him through thick and gin.

One who divorces his wife because she has a sobering effect on him; she hides the bottle.

BOSS

A person whom a man can put in good humor—by doing the dishes for her.

BRAT

A kid who behaves like your own, but belongs to a neighbor.

BRIDE

A woman who is carried over the threshold and immediately puts her foot down.

A female who has succeeded in getting a wedlock on a man.

A well-groomed girl who is leading an innocent man to the halter.

A woman who has exchanged the attentions of a lot of men for the inattention of one.

A female who is going from lipstick to broomstick.

An unsuspecting woman with an excellent prospect of happiness—behind her.

A girl who is well-groomed at a wedding.

Child Bride: A young female going right from homework to housework.

BRIDEGROOM

A wolf whose whistle got stuck.

The thing that is used at weddings.

A fellow who began by handing out a line, and ended up walking it.

A Prince Charming who doesn't suspect that he'll never become a ruler.

Bashful Bridegroom: A fellow who takes mistletoe along on his honeymoon.

A Potpourri of Definitions

BRIDE'S FATHER

A man who is losing a daughter but gaining a bathroom and a phone.

The man at the wedding who can't help shedding a few cheers.

BUDGET

A family's attempt to live beyond its yearnings.

A constant family struggle to keep up appearances and keep down expenses.

A domestic quarrel.

A household estimate of income and expenses, of which there is usually too much month left at the end of it.

A family's orderly system of living beyond its means.

A sure way to save money. By the time you have it figured up at night, it's too late to go anyplace.

BURIED TREASURE

A rich, deceased husband.

C

CAPABILITY

The quality that will get you to the top if the boss has no daughter.

CAPITAL PUNISHMENT

What a woman gets for marrying a government employee in Washington.

CAREER WOMAN

A working wife who would rather bring home the bacon than fry it.

One who prefers to go out as an employee than stay home and be a boss.

One who goes out and earns a man's salary, instead of sitting at home and taking it away from him.

CAVEMAN

A man who gets one hug from his wife and caves in.

CHANCE REMARK

Anything a man can manage to say when his wife and another woman are talking.

CHASTITY

The purity of a woman who has never been tempted.

CHECKMATE

A woman a man marries for her money.

CHICKEN

What many a man runs after, only to find it a wild goose chase.

CHILDISH GAME

One in which your wife can beat you.

CHILD PSYCHOLOGY

What parents use in letting their children have their own way.

CHILDREN

Young persons who grow by leaps and bounds—especially in the apartment overhead.

A Potpourri of Definitions

The family ask force.

Human gimme pigs.

Young people who wonder why Dad gets gray and Mom gets blonder.

Sons or daughters who will be a great comfort to you in your old age—and help you reach it faster.

Unreasonable facsimiles.

The younger gineration.

The why's guys in every family.

Young persons more of whom would be on the right track if parents provided switching facilities.

Natural mimics who behave like their parents in spite of every effort to teach them good manners.

The clear proof that insanity is hereditary. Parents get it from them.

Youngsters you pay an allowance for the privilege of living with them.

Young persons who are often bad because their parents did not burn their britches behind them.

Offspring who could get ahead if their parents pulled a few wires—the hi-fi wire, the radio wire, the television wire.

Kids whose parents are always worried how they will turn out, and who, in their turn, wonder when their parents will turn in.

Youngsters who are often spoiled because you can't spank two grandmothers.

Misbehaving Children: Youngsters whose parents embarked on the sea of matrimony without a paddle.

Problem Children: A misnomer. There are only children with problems.

CHIVALRY

The attitude of a man to any woman not his wife.

CO-ED

A sweater with a high I.Q.

A girl who may be poor on history, but great on dates.

A college girl whose chief objective is to graduate with a Magna Cum Lad.

COEDUCATIONAL INSTITUTE

The institution of marriage—and the hardest one to get through.

COFFEE CUP

One in which, in the estimation of many husbands, there are enough grounds for divorce.

COMBAT FATIGUE

The weariness of an oft-married person.

COMBAT JACKET

A garment a wife had to fight for to get.

COMMUTER

A man whose life is largely spent riding to and from his wife.

COMPATIBILITY

One that is based on mutual likes and dislikes, as when a man and wife both like to fight and both dislike each other.

A Potpourri of Definitions

COMPLIMENT

What a man pays a woman when he marries her, and it's usually the last.

Something which a husband and wife say to each other, and which both know is not true.

COMPROMISE

Where a wife can't stand her husband's ways, but stays married to him for his means.

A deal in which a married couple get what neither of them wanted.

CONSCIENCE

The inner voice that warns you that your mate is looking.

The thing that makes you tell your wife before somebody else does.

CONSERVATIVE

A man with a good job, a wife, several children, and a mortgaged home.

COQUETTE

A woman, after all.

One with a talent for womaneuvers.

A female whose sex appeal springs from her eye-cue.

One whose best-years-of-her-life are figured in man-hours.

COSMETICS

Beauty preparations used by a wife to keep her husband from reading between the lines.

COUNTERBALANCE

When a woman buys a fur coat for herself in a department store and a new hat for her husband.

COURAGE

Marrying a three-times-widowed woman.

COURTING

Wooing. The future tense of this word is "caught."

COURTSHIP

Love's sweet dream, followed by marriage—the alarm clock.

The wooing of a woman when a man whispers sweet nothings, and which ends when he says nothing sweet.

When a man murmurs that he isn't good enough for the girl, followed by marriage, when the girl mutters how right he was.

A quest; followed by marriage—the conquest; and divorce—the inquest.

The lipstick period; as distinguished from marriage, the broomstick period.

Spooning around with a cute dish; followed by marriage and forking over.

The period during which a girl is deciding whether she can get someone better.

The period when a man thinks he may be rejected, but the woman is spurning him on.

An animated introduction to a wearisome play.

The period when love makes time pass; as distinguished from marriage, when time often makes love pass.

A Potpourri of Definitions

The portion of time long enough for a man to chase a woman until she catches him.

The period during which a girl strings a fellow along only to see if he's fit to be tied.

CRYING
Tear-shedding, to which women resort to get things out of their systems, but more often out of their husbands.

CUPID
The well-known marksman with a bow and arrow, but one who has made some pretty bad Mrs.

The winged being who tries to make a hit with a miss, but many a miss complains that his hit was a bad miss.

The blind symbol of love.

Also known as Dan Cupid, although some husbands think it should be spelled with an *M*.

D

DATE
An appointment by two explorers for a joint expedition, often with wholly different destinations in mind.

DEAD-LETTER OFFICE
A husband's pocket.

DEAF-AND-DUMB COUPLE
The only married couple who can settle a quarrel at night by turning out the lights.

DECISION
What a man makes when he chooses to get married—and it's the last one he'll be allowed to make.

DELEGATE-AT-LARGE

A lucky fellow who can get away to a convention without his wife.

DELINQUENTS

Children who act like their parents.

DESERTION

The poor man's recourse in lieu of a divorce proceeding.

DESTITUTE

A word often spelled "dresstitute" by women.

DIAMOND

A stepping-stone to marriage.

DICTIONARY

The only place where divorce comes before marriage.

DIET

Your wife's art of sylph-defense, and letting the hips fall where they sway.

DIMPLE

Something many a man falls in love with, then makes the mistake of marrying the whole girl.

DINNER TABLE

Where families nowadays count their calories instead of their blessings.

DIPLOMAT

A husband who can bring home the bacon without spilling the beans.

A *Potpourri of Definitions*

One who calls his skinny wife "fashionably slender."

One who calls his fat wife "pleasingly plump."

One who calls his inarticulate wife "taciturn."

One who calls his gossiping wife a "brilliant conversationalist."

A man who can convince his wife she looks fat in a fur coat.

A man who can convince his wife that he hired a sexy-looking secretary because of her stenographic ability.

A man who remembers his wife's birthdays but forgets her age.

DISCRETION

When you are absolutely sure you are right and then ask your wife.

DISH TOWEL

The cloth that invariably wipes that contented look off a husband's face.

DISILLUSIONMENT

What happens when your son asks you to help him with his algebra.

DISTANT RELATIVE

Your husband's or wife's uncle who has money.

The most desirable kind to have—and the farther the better.

DIVORCE

A parting word.

(See Part II, Section 5 for definitions to end all definitions of divorce.)

DOMESTIC HELP

Something a woman no longer hires; she marries it.

DON'T

The best advice to give a man who is trying to win an argument with his wife.

DREAMS

What many people believe in, until they marry.

E

EATING

A favorite device among henpecked husbands to enable them to open their mouths.

EARLY BIRD

A husband who gets up to serve his wife breakfast in bed.

ECHO

The only thing that can cheat a garrulous wife out of the last word.

A name given to a wife who just must have the last word.

EFFICIENCY EXPERT

One whose wife, if she did what he does in his work, would be called a nagger.

EGOTIST

Any man who thinks that a woman married him for himself alone.

ELEVATOR OPERATOR

The only man who can tell his wife where to get off.

A Potpourri of Definitions

EMBRACE

What a girl gives a man before marriage. After marriage she puts the squeeze on him.

ENGAGEMENT

An option on a life sentence.

The period of urge on the verge of a merge.

A period of betrothal during which both parties wonder if they could do better.

The soothing stillness before the storm.

One time when a woman does not mind being placed in solitaire confinement.

ENGAGEMENT RING

A token of betrothal or marriage, the hardest part of which is paying for it.

An expensive buy-product of betrothal when given to a girl who is not stone-blind.

ETERNAL TRIANGLE

Family income, overhead, and upkeep.

EUPHONY

The agreeable sound of a woman's voice when she stops tongue-lashing her husband to answer the phone.

EVOLUTION

The process by which today's housewife has gone from dishpan hands to push-button fingers.

The theory that man descended from monkeys, which many people don't believe until they marry and meet their in-laws.

EXECUTIVE

A fellow who is a big noise in his place of business, but just a little squeak at home.

One who, if given enough rope, gets tied up at the office with his blond secretary.

EXHIBITIONIST

A girl wearing an engagement ring for the first time.

EXPERIENCE

That which teaches a man to tell his wife the truth the second time.

What a divorced couple have left after they have lost each other.

EXPERT

A married man away from home.

EXPLANATION

Something to give your wife at 3 A.M.

F

FAILURE

A man who may be one because his wife thinks he is.

FAIRY TALE

A story used to please a child or to fool a suspicious wife.

FAITHFUL

An adjective which describes a mother-in-law. She never goes home, no matter what her son-in-law does or says.

A Potpourri of Definitions

FALLEN WOMAN

A mother who neglected to pick up the kids' toys.

FALL-OUT SHELTER

A home in which a couple have been divorced.

FAMILY

The thing most needed nowadays in the home.

Large Family: The proof that married folks love children—or something.

FAMILY ALBUM

A book of pictures which can convince anyone that truth is an awful thing.

FAMILY LIFE

A case of perpetual commotion.

FAMILY MAN

A man who doesn't get a chance to read the Sunday newspaper until Monday night.

One who has several snapshots in his wallet where currency used to be.

A man who has several mouths to feed—and listen to.

The head of the family who worries about the outcome of his income because of the outgo for the upkeep.

FAMILY TREE

The tree that always produces some nuts.

FATHER

The kin you love to touch.

The man who was destined to be a banker.

FATHER *(Continued)*

The man in the family who is neither seen nor heard.

The person who can't get into the bathroom, on the phone, or out of the house.

One for whom the bills toll.

A man cruelly compelled to endure childbirth without the aid of an anesthetic.

One who, just about the time he gets his daughter off his hands, has to start putting his son-in-law on his feet.

Doting Father: One whose biggest worry is a dating daughter.

FATHER'S DAY

The same as Mother's Day, except he doesn't get nearly as much.

The day when he goes broke giving the family money so they can surprise him with gifts.

The special day when Junior allows you to wear that new necktie first.

A race between wife and children for the "surprise" gift that always ends in a tie—a necktie, leaving him fit to be tied.

The special occasion when dad gets a few small gifts and a lot of large bills from Mother's Day.

When dad gets a present that makes his eyes pop—a shirt with a collar two sizes too small for him.

FILIBUSTER

A talkative spouse's idea of conversation.

A Potpourri of Definitions

FINANCIAL GENIUS

One who can earn money faster than his family can spend it.

A man who can keep his wife from discovering how much money he makes and has.

One who has received a salary raise and his wife hasn't found out about it.

FINANCIAL SECURITY

Being able to cache some money where your wife won't find it.

FLATFOOT

A husband whose feet are in another woman's flat.

FLATTERY

The art of pretending you like the girl more than the kiss.

A flattering compliment, such as a wife demanding equal rights.

FLOWERS

A gift brought by men to their wives to accompany a weak alibi.

FOOL

A husband who tells his wife everything.

FOOTBALL SEASON

When a fellow can walk around with a girl on one arm and a blanket on the other without arousing suspicion.

FORBIDDEN FRUIT

Something that gets many a girl into a bad jam.

FORTUNE HUNTER

A chap who married a girl for her pa value.

One who is always on the lookout for a laborsaving device—a rich wife.

A man who marries a rich widow, and gives her everything her money can buy.

A fellow looking for a marriage-minded woman with a nice figure—like $100,000.

One who loves the ground his wife walks on, especially the real estate she owns.

FORTY

The ideal age for a wife—especially if she's fifty.

FREEDOM

The personal liberty which enables a man to do just what his wife pleases.

FREETHINKER

Any man who isn't married.

FUR

Sable, ermine, mink, beaver—as in the saying "Faint heart ne'er won fur, lady."

G

GENIUS

A father who can help his kids do their homework.
A creative, brilliant husband who can do everything except make a good living.

A *Potpourri* of Definitions

The outstandingly intelligent son in the family who needs several undistinguished brothers to support him.

Another woman's husband.

GENTLEMAN

One who when his wife drops something kicks it over to where she can pick it up more easily.

A man who steadies the stepladder for his wife while she paints the kitchen ceiling.

A man who never beats his wife without provocation.

GIGOLO

One who thinks women owe him a loving.

A fellow who earns his keep by heart labor.

A well-kept fee-male.

A chap who always carries a touch.

GIRL

A young woman whose maiden aim is to change her maiden name.

A young unmarried woman who wants to go with every Tom, Dick—and marry.

A female who's like a baseball player—always trying to turn a single into a double.

One whose ambition is the same as her mother's was—to make some man a good husband.

A miss with an inborn talent for convincing a fellow that his intentions are serious.

GIRL *(Continued)*

A young female who is eager to grow up and wear the kind of shoes and girdles that are killing Mother.

Bachelor girl: One who chooses to remain single while other girls would rather knot.

Modern girl: One who, while waiting for the right man to come along, is having a wonderful time with the wrong ones.

Nice girl: A gal who is known by the sweet nothing-doings she whispers in men's ears.

Smart girl: One who knows the difference between being bitten by a lovebug and a louse.

Working girl: One who quit her job to get married.

GIRLS

Females of two kinds: those who wish to get married, and those who haven't the slightest desire not to.

GO-GETTER

A man whose wife has a good job, and who makes sure on payday to go get 'er.

One who married a shrew and was sorry he got 'er.

GRANDCHILDREN

A son's or daughter's children, who don't make a man feel as old as the thought that he's married to a grandmother.

GRANDPARENTS

People who come to your house and spoil your children.

GREAT BEYOND

A family living beyond its income.

A Potpourri of Definitions

GREAT GUY

Your wife's first husband, or the fellow she might have married.

GRINDSTONE

What some men keep their noses to so their wives can turn theirs up at the neighbors.

GROUCH

A sick husband.

H

HAPPY FAMILY

One in which children are properly spaced—about ten feet apart.

HARD LOSER

Any spouse on a diet.

HAT

The atrocity worn by your wife that leaves no doubt who wears the plants in the family.

HEREDITY

What parents believe in until their children act like fools.

HERO

A married man.

HIGH FIDELITY

A chronic tippler who goes home regularly to his wife.

HIS

A pronoun meaning "hers."

HOBBY

A man's favorite occupation, which may not drive him crazy, but the same can't be said for his family.

What a man claims he has after dinner to avoid having to help his wife with the dishes.

HOLLYWOOD

Cinemaland, where the movies are running longer and the marriages are running shorter.

A place where, if an actor's wife looks like a new woman, she probably is.

HOME

The abode from which on a clear day you can see the finance company.

The place you stay at while the car is being repaired.

The place where a switch regulates everything except the kids.

Where the man of the family can say what he likes because no one pays the scantest attention to him.

A place where nowadays the thing most needed in it is the family.

Where the mortgage is.

Where the parents watch the Late, Late Show while sitting up waiting for their children to come home.

A residence with wall-to-wall windows, wall-to-wall carpeting, and back-to-the-wall financing.

A Potpourri of Definitions

The family's filling station.

Where everyone in the family thinks nothing of taking off their new shoes and putting on their old manners.

Where a sixteen-hour-a-day wife works for an eight-hour-a-day husband.

The place where members of a family put up with each other.

What people buy expensive furniture for, and then buy cars to get away from it.

HOME COOKING
Where a man hopes his wife is.

A can-glomeration.

Which makes many husbands complain that they never thaw such meals as their wives serve.

Prepared food which a married man would have if his wife was.

HOMEMADE MEALS
Meals that often drive husbands away from home.

HOME OWNER
One who can always be found on his way to a hardware store.

HOMESICK
An inclination to be sick of one's home.

HONEYMOON
That blissful period of married life which is over when:

Necking changes to pecking.

HONEYMOON (Continued)

A man takes his wife off a pedestal, and puts her on a budget.

The husband stops wearing his toupee around the house.

The bride who thought she was mad about you is just mad at you.

You don't notice that your wife is wearing a new dress until you get a bill for it.

The dog brings your slippers and your wife barks at you.

Your wife no longer cares whether you get home late.

The vacation a man takes before going to work for a new boss.

The period that soon ends when the husband stops helping his wife with the dishes and does them by himself.

Second honeymoon: The pleasurable period following the wedding, providing it's with a different wife.

HORSE SENSE

Stable thinking which enables a man to stay away from a nag.

HOSPITAL

An establishment for the care of husbands who strike their wives.

A place where run-down husbands usually wind up.

HOUSEKEEPER

An old-fashioned wife.

A Potpourri of Definitions

HOUSEKEEPER (of a sort)

A wife who is a rarely good cook—very rarely.

One who is shocked when her husband utters a four-letter word—like "Cook!"

A married woman whose closets would be messy even if she lived in a nudist camp.

One who, so far as household chores are concerned, likes to do nothing better.

One who keeps plugging in this age of automation.

A woman who is an expert at slighting the housework where it doesn't show.

One whose husband brings home the bacon, and she burns it.

A wife who thinks her work was done when she swept down the aisle.

One who can dish it out but can't cook it.

A cute little dish who isn't too keen to be a cute little dishwasher.

One who will put on almost anything for dinner, except an apron.

A woman who keeps her promise to her husband to keep her kitchen immaculate; they eat out.

HOUSEWARMING

The last call for wedding presents.

HOUSEWORK

The main reason why women go out looking for a job.

HUG

A roundabout way of manifesting your love.

HUSBAND

A spousebroken individual.

(See Part II, Section 3 for definitions to end all definitions of husbands.)

HYPNOTISM

Getting a man in your power; like marriage, for instance.

HYPOCHONDRIACAL SPOUSE

One whose life is constantly a bed of neuroses.

One with a malady that keeps malingering on.

A mate who always gives you a grief resume.

A man who won't kiss his wife unless her lipstick has penicillin in it.

One who always gives her husband a preamble to her constitution.

A manic-depressive mate—the easy glum, easy glow type.

A husband or wife who just can't leave being well enough alone.

HYPOCRITE

A man who hands his pay to his wife with a smile on his face.

I

IDEAL WORLD

One where all the women are married, and all men are bachelors.

A Potpourri of Definitions

IDEAS

Conceptions or notions. There are really only two ideas in the world; men have one and women the other.

ILLEGITIMATE CHILD

A sinfant.

One descended from a long line its mother listened to.

INCOMPATIBILITY

Frequently a situation where the husband has no income and the wife isn't pattable.

INFIDELITY

The application of democracy to marriage.

INITIATIVE

Enterprise which a married man may have, but his wife has the referendum.

IN-LAW

A relative by marriage, often regarded as an outlaw.

INSANITY

A hereditary derangement which parents get from their children.

A mental derangement which is not only a ground for annulment, but frequently for marriage as well.

INSEPARABLE

A couple so joined together that it takes a couple of cops or neighbors to pull them apart.

INSTALLMENT PLAN

A system by which many things are bought for the house with a dollar down, and the balance in uneasy payments.

INTIMATE RESTAURANT

Where the boss takes his wife when he doesn't want his secretary to see them.

INTUITION

A wife's ability to read between her husband's lyin's.

The quality that enables your wife to put two and two together and come up with any answer that suits her.

The ability of a woman to contradict her husband before he has a chance to say anything about the subject.

The unique instinct which tells your wife that she is right, whether she is or not.

That sixth sense that allows a married woman to make five wrong guesses.

The innate quality that makes it possible for a wife to size up a situation in a flash of misunderstanding.

Your wife's built-in radar.

Another name for a wife's suspicion.

A woman's attribute, which is often mistaken for her husband's transparency.

The infallible instinct by which a wife puts two and two together and gets her husband's number.

INVOICE

The only voice the head of the family has regarding the things that are bought for the home.

IRONY

Giving father a billfold for Christmas.

J

JEALOUSY

The uneasiness of an insecure mate.

The mark of a spouse who has more self-love than love.

JILT

What a fellow does when he buys a girl a wedding gown, and then gives her the slip.

JOINT BANK ACCOUNT

Where the husband puts the money in, and the wife takes it out.

JUNE

The favorite month for weddings—full of perfect daze.

The month when a well-groomed girl looks at the bride side of life with a Lohengrin on her face.

The popular month for weddings, followed by the other eleven for divorces.

The month of weddings and cooings, after which the billing follows the cooing.

JUNGLE WARFARE

A contested divorce suit.

JUVENILE DELINQUENCY

The result of parents trying to train children without starting at the bottom.

K

KISSING

A caress of the lips which shortens life—single life.

A contraction of a spouse's mouth which is not always accompanied by an enlargement of the heart.

A two-faced action that it worthwhile if indulged in by mates who are not two-faced.

A lip service to married love, yet not enough if it is only lip service.

What a man who seldom kisses his wife resents when another man kisses her.

A heart-quake.

Something a man can't believe a woman understands until he has it from her own lips.

A word that has two S's because it requires two to finish the spell.

A course of procedure cunningly devised for the mutual stoppage of conversation at a moment when words are superfluous.

Kiss and make up: Where the girl gets the kiss and the fellow gets the makeup.

KITCHEN

The room for which wives have discovered a marvelous method for keeping it spotlessly clean. It's called "eating out."

The place in which life is one canned thing after another.

A Potpourri of Definitions

Where a husband can always tell when they're having salad for dinner; he doesn't smell anything burning.

KITCHENETTE

A small kitchen designed by the same person who made the telephone booth.

L

LADY

One who when she says No means Perhaps. When she says Perhaps she means Yes. But if she says Yes she's no lady.

LANDED GENTRY

Men who are either engaged or married.

LAW

What a man lays down to his wife, but which is repealed by her.

Principles of government whose majesty somehow always seems to be in favor of Her Majesty.

LEISURE

The heavenly hour's rest a man manages to get when his wife doesn't think up something for him to do.

LIEUTENANT COMMANDER

A lieutenant's wife.

LIFE

A marry chase.

LITTLE ROCK

The state capital that many women think of when they look at their engagement rings.

LONGEVITY

A long life sought for attainment by men who have to live long enough to do all the things their wives want them to do.

LOUDSPEAKER SYSTEM

A device appropriately donated by a man to a church in memory of his late wife.

LOVE

Something the minister throws in with "Honor" and "Obey."

(*See Part II, Section 2 for definitions to end all definitions of love.*)

LUXURY

Anything a husband needs.

LYING

A practice of husbands which could be cut down considerably if wives did not ask so many questions.

M

MAGICIAN

A husband or wife who can turn anything into an argument.

MAN

Homo sapiens, who has two periods in life when he does not understand women: before marriage and after marriage.

The creature who is merely dust, and a wife settles him.

One who knever knows the real meaning of bliss until he gets married, and then it's too late.

A species of the second-toughest sex.

A Potpourri of Definitions

The forgotten creature: When he's born, people ask, "How's the mother doing?" When he marries, they say, "Isn't the *bride* lovely!" When he dies, they ask, "How much did he leave her?"

A member of the unthought-of, or insignificant sex.

Long-whiskered man: One with a wife, a couple of daughters, and only one bathroom.

Man of the Hour: Any man whose wife tells him to wait "just a couple of minutes."

Man's dangerous age: Any time between one and ninety-one.

Man's imagination: The mental image or concept of a woman, which is her chief asset.

Second-story man: One who is always ready with a second story if his wife does not believe the first one.

Self-made man: One whose wife has made a few alterations.

One who can't blame it on his wife.

Successful man: Often one who owes his prosperity to his first wife, and his second wife to his prosperity.

One who can earn more than his family can spend.

A fellow who had to make more money to meet the obligations he wouldn't have had if he hadn't married.

One whose wife drove him to distinction.

MARRIAGE

A word that is not a word, but a sentence.

(*See Section 2 for definitions to end all definitions of marriage.*)

MARTYR

A man who lives up to his wife's expectations of him.

One who has told his wife the honest-to-goodness truth without her believing a word of it.

MATCH FACTORY

A co-ed college.

MATE

The kind you dream about—and the kind you marry.

MATERNAL LOVE

A strong affection for children that is often smotherly love.

MATERNITY DRESS

A space suit.

A magical frock that makes the heir unapparent.

MATRIMONY

The first union to defy management.

Where a man goes to adore, rings a belle, gives his name to a maid, and then is taken in.

School of Matrimony: One in which too many pupils learn too late.

MEMORY

The mental faculty which reminds a man that his wedding anniversary was the day before.

MEMORY EXPERT

A woman who has once been told her sister-in-law's right age.

A Potpourri of Definitions

MIDDLE AGE

What you first notice in your spouse.

When your husband's age starts to show around the middle.

The destiny that ends your mate's shape.

MILLINERY

Your wife's hatrocities.

MINK COAT

Something you give your wife to keep her warm or quiet.

MINORITY

A man with a wife and a couple of teen-age children.

MINUTEMAN

A man whose wife can shut him up in a minute.

MISSING PERSONS' BUREAU

Where people should apply if they're looking for perfect mates.

MISTAKE

Something that all folks make—only married people learn about them sooner.

The best way to tell your wife's age.

MISTRESS

A q.t. cutie.

The "other woman," who takes the place of a wife, except that you don't have to help with the dishes.

MIXED EMOTIONS
Watching your mother-in-law go over a cliff in your new car.

MODERN HITCHING-POST
The third finger of a woman's left hand.

MODERN PARENT
One who has to spare the rod so that Junior can ride in it.

MONOGAMY
Proof that the law protects men who are incapable of protecting themselves.

The same as bigamy, which is having one wife too many.

A system cleverly originated by wives to make their husbands believe what they say about other women.

A non-harem-forming practice.

MONOLOGUE
A conversation between a husband and wife.

A mate's idea of conversation that is frequently a moanalogue or a monopologue.

MOON
The heavenly body that affects not only the tied, but the untied.

The celestial body which once inspired only romance instead of space travel.

MORTAL ENEMY
The guy who runs away with your wife—and then brings her back.

A Potpourri of Definitions

MOTHER

A woman who constantly causes her daughter to wonder where she learned all those things she tells her not to do.

One who wonders how, if it took her twenty years to make a man of her boy, it took another woman twenty minutes to make a fool of him.

A woman whose life is disorganized around her children.

Modern mother:

One who can hold a safety pin, a bobby pin, and a cigarette in her mouth all at the same time.

A female whose only thing found at her knees nowadays is her skirt.

Mother's Day: Nine months after Father's Day.

Mother of ten: A woman who has gone stork-mad.

Unwed mother: A girl who surrenders, without benefit of wedlock, to a boyological urge.

MOTHER-IN-LAW

A woman who visits only twice a year, and stays six months each visit.

The matrimonial kin that gets under your skin.

A talkie that has come to stay.

A husband's or wife's mother whose condition is fair to meddling.

A mother-in-awe.

Another mouth to heed.

MOTHER-IN-LAW *(Continued)*

A woman who thinks marriage is a good investment if she puts her two cents in.

One who feels that the "in-law" designation qualifies her to lay down the law.

One who believes that three can live as cheaply as two.

A person who is never outspoken.

An umpire with a partiality toward one of the fighters.

One whose gift from her son-in-law is usually a jar of vanishing cream.

A woman whose daughter-in-law gets along all right with her because she can't afford another baby-sitter.

Grouchy mother-in-law: No laughing mater.

MUMBLE

All a couple need to do with a few words to get married in church, or with a few in their sleep to get divorced.

MYSTERY

The great unexplained secret so far as husbands are concerned: what a bachelor does with his money.

N

NAG

A wife without horse sense.

One who mistakes the right of free speech for free screech.

A Potpourri of Definitions

A wife who tames to be pleased.

A man's booin' companion.

A woman who marries a man with the object of giving him a new leash on life.

A wife who is all peaches and scream.

A womanacle.

NAME-DROPPING
What a single girl wishes concerning her maiden name.

NECESSITY
Any luxury a family can afford.

NEEDLE
Something easier to find in a haystack than in a modern wife's hand.

NEWLYWED
A man who tells his wife when he gets a salary raise.

Unhappy newlyweds: The moaning after the night before.

NEWSPAPER
A publication that prints marriage and death notices on the same page in the belief that sorrows never come singly.

NOBODY'S FOOL
Someone who has just gotten a divorce.

NURSING A GROUCH
What a wife does when she's attending a sick husband.

O

OLD MAID

A female without a gent to her name.

A female whose father never owned a shotgun.

A woman who knows all the answers, but isn't asked the question.

One with a wait problem.

Old maid's giggle: He! He! He!

OPTIMIST

A man who asks his wife to help him with the dishes.

A man who marries his secretary thinking he'll continue to dictate to her.

A bridegroom.

A bigamist.

A married man who expects his wife to be a sweetheart, domestic servant, wet nurse, and audience.

A person who thinks cynics and quipsters will eventually run out of definitions of marriage.

One who expects the Internal Revenue Service to believe his statement on his tax return that he is head of the house.

A chap who thinks his wife has quit smoking cigarettes when he finds cigar butts around the house.

A person who marries a pessimist.

A man who believes his wife when she threatens to go home to mother.

A *Potpourri of Definitions*

A man who marries at seventy, and looks for a home near a school.

ORGANIZED CHARITY

A husband's or wife's relatives.

OURS

A word usually found missing in unsuccessful marriages.

P

PAR

What a golf addict's children call their father.

PARENTS

People who beget infants, bore teen-agers, and board newlyweds.

People who think their children would behave if they didn't play with the kids next door.

Persons one-half of whose lives have been ruined by their parents, and the other half is being ruined by their children.

Folks whose children would be smarter if they smarted in the right places.

People who need more than understanding to be pals to their children—it needs stamina.

Folks for whom the economic law reverses to Demand and Supply.

Fathers and mothers who are afraid to put their feet down for fear of having their toes stepped on.

PARENTS (*Continued*)

A name for people who practice the rhythm system of birth control.

Modern parents: People who cut rugs instead of switches.

PEDAL PUSHERS

What your wife wears when you can't decide whether she looks worse in slacks or Bermuda shorts.

PEDESTRIAN

A fellow whose wife beat him to the car.

A man who won't provide his family with a second car.

A man who counted on his wife to put some gas in the car.

PENTHOUSE

An apartment preferred by folks who enjoy high living.

PERFECTION

Something only found in bachelors' wives and old maids' children.

PHILOSOPHER

What a man becomes when he gets married.

PLEASURE TRIP

Driving your mother-in-law back home.

POETIC JUSTICE

When a man who'd rather play golf than eat, marries a woman who'd rather play cards than cook.

POISE

The quality of a wife who can get her way by raising an eyebrow instead of the roof.

A Potpourri of Definitions

POLYGAMY

Having several wives, as distinguished from bigamy—having two wives—and monotony—one wife.

A practice that's fast becoming obsolete in the United States—impossible to imagine several women in a modern kitchenette.

POOR FISH

A fellow who gets hooked with his own line.

POOR LOSER

A wife on a diet.

POSTSCRIPT

The supplementary part of a woman's letter, which is like the shifty small print in a contract.

PRACTICAL NURSE

One who marries a rich patient.

PRESENT

A gift a man receives from his wife shortly before he receives the bill.

PROPOSAL

When a man is so overcharged with emotion he can hardly speak, but realizes after marriage that he was too loquacious and expressive.

Modern proposal: Popping the question without questioning the pop.

PSYCHIATRIST

A practitioner, half of whose patients go to him because they aren't married, while the other half go to him because they are.

A person who asks you a lot of expensive questions that your wife asks for nothing.

PSYCHOLOGY

A wife's sigh-chological process.

PUZZLEMENT

Bafflement or perplexity; created by questions such as, "If ignorance is bliss, why aren't there more happy married couples?"

Why a woman without any horse sense is called a nag.

Why they draft married men, when they have no fight left in them.

Why, if weddings are supposed to be happy occasions, the groom wears black.

Why, if a wife's intuition is so good, she always has to ask questions.

Why every bachelor isn't a millionaire.

Whether men who like to cook practice it as a hobby, or for self-preservation.

What line Eve used, since she couldn't throw up to Adam the better men she could have married.

Why a woman will look into a mirror any time, except when she's pulling out of a parking space.

A Potpourri of Definitions

How the boy who wasn't good enough to marry the daughter can be the father of the smartest grandchild in the world.

Why it takes women today as much time to get dressed as it did when they wore clothes.

What women found attractive about men before money was invented.

Why familes buy homes, and then buy cars to get away from them.

Why love at first sight is considered so remarkable. It's when a couple can look at each other for years that it becomes remarkable.

When two wives get together, who gets the last word.

Why couples who can read each other like a book, can't shut each other up like one.

Why, when a man says something silly, people say, "Isn't he silly!" But when a woman does, they say, "Aren't women silly!"

R

REDUCING SALON

A place that takes your wife's breadth away.

RELAXATION

The brief rest a man gets while his wife is thinking up something else for him to do.

REMARRIAGE

The triumph of hope over experience.

RENO

Where a man goes for a change of wife.

Temporary residence of the bitter half.

The American inland seaport notable for the tied running in and the untied running out.

The parting-of-the-ways place in our democracy for couples for whom democracy has failed to work.

The land of the free and the grave of the home.

Sue City.

Convenient grounds for divorce.

The place where disturbed people go to be reno-vated.

REVENGE

The vindictive act of a woman who gets even with her husband by staying married to him.

RICE

Something that some couples hate because it's associated with the biggest mistake of their lives.

RINGLEADER

The first in a large family to take a bath on a Saturday night.

ROMANCE

A dreamy amour that begins with sentiment and ends with a settlement.

Something that begins with an ocean of emotion and winds up in marriage with an expanse of expense.

A Potpourri of Definitions

A love affair that begins like a violin with beautiful music, but with unconcern that the strings are still attached in marriage.

A form of *neck*romancy.

The only sport in which the animal that gets caught has to buy the license.

An affair that often begins out in the country with a pint of corn, and ends up with a full crib.

Football romance: One in which one or both parties are waiting for the other to kick off.

Garden romance: A dead-beat married to an old tomato.

Ideal romance: One in which a couple get married and live happily *even* afterward.

S

SAFE-AND-SANE FOURTH

One desired by a woman who's had three husbands who were either worthless or batty.

SALARY

What a man commands and his wife commandeers.

SCRAPBOOK

A book which is often the diary of a quarrelsome couple.

SENSE OF HUMOR

What people often show in their choice of mates.

The ability to laugh at your own jokes when your wife tells them.

SENSE OF HUMOR (Continued)

Something God kept from women so they could love their husbands instead of laughing at them.

SEPTUAGENARIAN

One who doesn't care where his wife goes, just so he doesn't have to go with her.

SHADY CHARACTER

A fellow who snoozes in a hammock under a tree while his wife mows the lawn.

SHATTERED NERVES

What a wife has when her husband talks indistinctly in his sleep.

SHOTGUN WEDDING

A case of wife or death.

SHOWER

Something understandable that no groom gets—to all intents and purposes he's all washed up anyway.

The beginning of the end of a man's reign.

SHREW

A woman who goes from "I do" to "You'd better not do."

A Mrs. who hisses her husband.

A female who thinks the wedding certificate is a driver's license.

One who even complains about the noise her husband makes when he fixes his own breakfast.

A woman who throws hisses instead of kisses.

A *Potpourri of Definitions*

A woman who handpicks her man before marriage, and henpecks him afterward.

One who gives her husband a piece of her mind, and takes away the peace of his.

SLEEP-TALK

The only talk of a spouse that gets the other's undivided attention.

SMALL TOWN

Where everyone knows which husbands beat their wives, but also which ones deserve it.

Where if you see a young woman dancing with a man old enough to be her father—he is.

Where if a woman sees a strange man entering her neighbor's house she goes over to borrow a cup of sugar.

Where everyone knows whose check is good and whose husband isn't.

SMILE

Something that adds to your mate's face value.

SMUGNESS

The complacent feeling a woman experiences when she sees a double chin on her husband's old girl friend.

SNORING

Domestic sheet music.

Something that makes a married person's life no bed of dozes.

SPEED

The rapidity with which a man drives his mother-in-law back to her own home.

SPOUSE

A former lover.

Cheerful spouse: A happychondriac.

Disillusioned spouse: One who remembers *when* he or she got married but not *why*.

Even-tempered spouse: One who is always mad.

Fickle spouse:

A husband or wife who is up to he- or she-nanigans.
One who believes the plural of spouse is spice.
One whose mate's absence makes the heart go wander.

Garrulous spouse:

One whose reasoning is largely sound.
One who, generally speaking, is generally speaking.
A mate with a nice open face—open day and night.
A husband or wife badly in need of a yappendectomy.
A freight train of wordage—with no terminal facilities.
One whose word is never done.

Ideal spouse: The one you're not married to.

Immature spouse: One who suffers from infantuation.

Neurotic spouse: One who not only expects the worst, but makes the worst of it when it happens.

Patient spouse: Merely one with a postponed temper.

Unfaithful spouse: One who moves in the best triangles.

SPRING

The time of the year when a young man's fancy lightly turns —to what a girl has been thinking about all winter.

A *Potpourri of Definitions*

The season when if a girl hasn't yet married she looks around for a fall guy.

SPRING-CLEANING

A process that explains to husbands why hurricanes are given female names.

STAG

A party to which husbands like to come without their dears.

STALEMATE

A husband who repeats the same joke ad infinitum.

STORK

The bird with the big bill.

The world's greatest kidder.

A bird often charged with something that should be blamed on a lark.

STRENGTH OF CHARACTER

The quality that is only called stubbornness by a man's family.

SUBURBANITE

A fellow who hires someone to mow his lawn so he can play golf for exercise.

SUCCESS

Something that comes quicker to the man your wife could have married.

SUITOR

A chap who thinks he's throwing a girl a line, while all the time he is being roped in.

SUMMER CAMP

A place where children go for their parents' vacation.

SURVIVAL KIT

A family man's wallet.

T

TEARS

The hydraulic force through which a husband's will-power is overpowered by his wife's waterpower.

TEEN-AGE BRIDE

A girl with a boyological urge going from homework to housework.

TEEN-AGE GIRL

One who would run away from home if she could get a long enough extension cord for the telephone.

TEEN-AGE MARRIAGE

Merged at an early urge.

TELEVISION

Proof that some married people would rather look at anything but each other.

TEMPER

What you call it in your spouse, but temperament in yourself.

TENDER

Something a wife adores about her husband—especially if it's legal tender.

A Potpourri of Definitions

THRILL

Getting married, and being able to thumb your nose at the hotel house detective.

THUMB

The short, thick inner digit on a woman's hand that has her husband under it.

TIN ANNIVERSARY

Celebrating five years of eating out of tin cans.

TOMBSTONE

A monumental lie about the virtues of a deceased spouse.

A stone placed over a husband's grave by a rich widow who doesn't believe in taking chances.

TOMORROW

A lazy husband's greatest laborsaving device.

TRADE RELATIONS

Something a lot of married folks would like to do.

TRIAL MARRIAGE

A vague term; all marriages are trial marriages.

TWIN BEDS

The things that make people walk in their sleep.

TWINS

Wombmates.

U

UNFORGETTABLE WOMAN

The ex-wife to whom you are paying alimony.

V

VACATION RESORT

Where girls go to look for husbands, and husbands go to look for girls.

VANITY

Parents trying to get their children to be like them.

VEGETARIAN

An apt nickname for a girl who goes out only with men with plenty of cabbage.

W

WAR DEBT

Alimony.

WATERPOWER

A wife's tears.

WEAK

What a man is when a woman cunningly tells him how strong he is.

A Potpourri of Definitions

WEAKER SEX

A misnomer.

Said to be women, but actually the stronger sex because of the weakness of the stronger sex for the weaker sex.

WEDDING

A ceremony sanguinely pledging two powers to coo-existence.

A funeral where you smell your own flowers.

A ritual before which the woman cries, and afterward the man.

A ceremony at which a man loses complete control of himself.

An event where they rope off the aisles so the groom can't get away.

A function where a man places a ring on a woman's third finger and himself under her thumb.

A public announcement of a strictly private intention.

A celebration where the bride finds it difficult to keep the triumphant look off her face.

Golden wedding: Proof that there are some couples with the stamina to fight it out to the finish.

Anniversary of a couple who would rather fight than switch.

The time when a couple can draw from sweet memories if they've made regular deposits.

Postponed wedding:

> One that is said to bring bad luck—unless it is postponed indefinitely.

Shotgun wedding:

> A case of troth or consequences.
>
> An "I do" or die affair.

WEDDING BELLS

A storm warning.

WEDDING GIFT

The alimony a wife gets after the divorce.

WEDDING KNOT

One that is supposed to tie a couple, but frequently merely entangles them.

WEDDING MARCH

A song that every girl can be had for.

The overture to divorce.

WEDDING REHEARSAL

Aisle trial.

WEDDING RING

A one-man band.

A tourniquet that stops a woman's circulation.

The world's smallest handcuff.

An exultant bride's war-hoop.

A Potpourri of Definitions

WEDDING VOW

To love, honor, and have children that disobey.

WEDLOCK

A padlock.

One in which there is often not enough wed and too much lock.

The lock that is supposed to fasten a couple together for life, but is too often forced open in a divorce court.

WELL-INFORMED

What a married man is whose wife has just told him what she thinks of him.

WHIM

The singular of women who are wives.

WIDOW

The proof that women live longer than men.

A woman who can be thankful for at least one thing—she always knows where her husband is.

An ex-dish jockey.

A woman from whom more can be learned than from an entire library of books on marriage.

One who has an advantage over other women. She knows all about men, and the only man who knows all about her can tell no tales.

A woman who expects her second husband to conform to the eulogistic inscription on her first husband's gravestone.

WIDOW *(Continued)*

One who would gladly give up $5,000 of the $50,000 insurance money her husband left her to have him back again.

A woman who may get over her first husband's death, but whose second husband may not.

One who, far from forgetting men, is for getting one as soon as possible.

Grass widow: One who is not necessarily green.

Lonesome widow: A woman looking for an electric blanket that snores.

Mourning widow: One who insists on black olives in her martinis.

Rich widow:

Second-hand goods that sells at first-class prices.

One who when her husband dies passes on to a better life.

Tearful widow: Often the kind who remarries quickly; wet weather is very convenient for transplanting.

WIDOWER

The only man who has an angel for a wife.

WIDOW-MAKERS

Husbands.

WIDOW'S WEEDS

The easiest to kill. You have only to say "Wilt thou?" and they wilt.

A Potpourri of Definitions

WIFE

A woman who gets bed and boredom.

(See Part II, Section 4 for definitions to end all definitions of wife.)

WILD OATS

A dissolute practice, sown by impulsive girls with the hope of crop failure.

WILLPOWER

A husband's faculty of deliberate action, which is no match for his wife's wile power.

WOMAN

A person who waits for the right man to come along, but in the meantime she gets married.

The weeper sex in the institution of marriage.

A husband's solace; but if it weren't for her, he wouldn't need any solace.

A delusion, but one that men are always hugging.

One whose weight cannot be told by her sighs.

A mistress of arts who robs a bachelor of his degree.

A person with a keen sense of humor—the more you humor her, the better.

A person who will waive some of her rights, but not her permanent wave.

A great booklover—provided it's filled with trading stamps.

WOMAN *(Continued)*

The female of the species who started out as a side issue, and has never been one since.

Man's problem—but the kind he apparently likes to wrestle with.

One who, by the time a man whispers, "We were made for each other," is already planning alterations.

A person who has a cleaner mind than a man because she changes it more often.

A creature who makes up her face more easily than she does her mind.

A fascinating topic. The correct understanding of her depends on the way a man grasps the subject.

Flighty woman: One whom a man finds very interesting while he's looking for a sensible, marriageable one.

Oft-married woman:

One who is able to build a better spouse-trap than other women.

A busybody.

One who has a wash-and-wear bridal gown.

A female who has been married so many times, wedding guests throw instant rice at her.

A woman who must be awfully fond of wedding cake.

One who marries in haste and repeats at pleasure.

Successful woman: One who is married to a successful man who earns more than she can spend.

A Potpourri of Definitions

WOMAN'S BRAIN

What a man looks for in a woman after he's looked at everything else.

WOMAN'S COLLEGE

An institution of higher yearning.

WOMAN-HATER

A man with a miss-shun in the world.

WOMEN'S CLUBS

Something husbands are in favor of, especially when kindness fails.

WOODEN ANNIVERSARY

The day folks realize what blockheads they were to get married.

WRING

What a girl does with her hands when she can't get one on her finger.

X

XMAS

The time when Santa Claus comes around with a bag, and leaves Dad holding it.

The season of the year when husbands and wives exchange sensible gifts—like ties and fur coats.

The time when both trees and husbands get lit up.

The time of the year when women get the children things for their fathers to play with.

Y

YAWN

Nature's providential device for letting a husband open his mouth.

YES

The answer to any question your wife asks.

YES-MAN

A married man who stoops to concur.

Something which married men aren't. When their wives say "No," they say "No."

YOUTHFUL FIGURE

What you get when you ask a woman her age.

Z

ZEAL

The fervor with which you leap on your spouse's shortcomings.

PART TWO

Definitions

A condition of the mind when the mind is out of condition.

A state of perpetual anesthesia. (*H. L. Mencken*)

A word made up of two vowels, two consonants, and two fools.

The association of two people for the benefit of one.

A lot of dame foolishness.

A gross exaggeration of the difference between one person and every body else. (*George Bernard Shaw*)

Something that begins with a fever and ends with a yawn.

A passion fancy.

The last word in a telegram.

A mutual misunderstanding. (*Oscar Wilde*)

The triumph of imagination over intelligence and of reflexes over reflection.

A tie that binds, as distinguished from matrimony, which straps them together.

Sentimental measles. (*Charles Kingsley*)

An ocean of emotions, entirely surrounded by expenses. (*Thomas Dewar*)

The only fire against which there is no insurance.

The star people look up to preceding the marital coal hole they fall into.

An attachment to one of the opposite sex induced by a need to escape from oneself.

Woman's eternal spring and man's eternal fall. (*Helen Rowland*)

The passionate affection which causes a woman without any sense to marry a man without any dollars.

The never-ending comedy of Eros.

An itch around the heart that many married folks wish they had been able to scratch.

A temporary insanity curable by marriage, or by removal of the patient from the influences under which he incurred the disorder. (*Ambrose Bierce*)

Love

The delusion that one woman differs from another. (*H. L. Mencken*)

The quest, as distinguished from marriage—the conquest—and divorce—the inquest.

The fanciful feeling of two changeable persons of the opposite sex that they will never change.

The dirty trick nature played on us to achieve the continuation of the species. (*W. Somerset Maugham*)

The thing that enables a woman to smile while she mops up the floor after her husband has walked across it in his muddy shoes.

The passionate attachment, which makes time pass, as distinguished from marriage, which makes love pass.

A crazy desire on the part of a chump to pay a woman's board and lodging bill for life.

The only known game which two can play and where both can win or lose.

The intoxication of life, as distinguished from marriage, the morning-after hangover.

One fool thing after another on the part of two fools after each other.

An attachment that men are only really all worked up about at the beginning, and women just before the end.

The offspring of illusion, and the parent of disillusion.

The self-deception that makes a person satisfied with only one member of the opposite sex.

A more conventional word for sexual desire.

The heartburn that often leads to a heartache.

The frequent case of a tongue's flattery leading to a heart's fluttery.

A combination of sex and sentiment. (*André Maurois*)

The more subtle form of self-interest. (*Holbrook Jackson*)

The rapturous feeling that makes a female make a male make a fool of himself.

The condition that gave rise to the proverb, "'Tis better to have loved and lost—much better."

The history of a woman's life; an episode in man's. (*Mme. de Staël*)

A state of affairs that has some compensations—alimony, for instance.

A force too great to be surmounted by anything but a hasty retreat.

A matter like eating mushrooms; you never know whether it's good for you until it's too late.

A delightful feeling, with the hitch occurring when the knot is tied.

An initially welcome heart attack that is only too often followed by a hardening of the hearteries.

Something resembling a dog chasing its tail. You can wear yourself out trying to catch something you couldn't get away from if you tried.

Not entirely a delirium, yet it has many points in common therewith. (*Thomas Carlyle*)

Propaganda for propagation.

Love

A blindness that owes its prevalence to the sense of touch.

A bit of sighing, a bit of crying, a bit of dying, and a good deal of lying.

A malady of the nervous system and the nymph glands.

The season pass on the shuttle between courtship and the divorce court.

A fire that should warm the hearth, but too often burns down the house.

A thing that foolish people think they can buy, but wind up paying heavily for it.

The feeling that makes two amorous people think almost as much of each other as they think of themselves.

A condition that manifests itself in four stages: calf love, half love, old love, and cold love.

A state of blindness, as distinguished from marriage—the eye-opener.

An emptiness that strikes first in the pit of the stomach, and finally winds up in the head.

A word that everyone uses, but defines for himself.

The thing that makes the heart light and the parlor dark.

A softening of the hearteries.

To a woman a breath of life, and to a man a passing zephyr.

The thing that lies in the sexes' eyes—and lies, and lies, and lies.

A sexual affection, during which Cupid makes you act stupid.

Something that is highly valued during the time when a man pays court, and even higher during his day in court.

The affection that enables a woman to forgive her husband for forgetting her birthday but remembering her age.

That which enables a woman to forgive her husband for getting theatre tickets in the last row over to the side.

LOVE AT FIRST SIGHT

A time-saver; but lots of married people wish they had wiped their glasses for a good second look.

LOVE BIRDS

Married couples that are always flying at each other.

LOVE LETTER

A noose paper.

An I and U that becomes an IOU in a breach-of-promise suit.

Ardent epistles which many sentimental women keep, and which some calculating women make sure will keep them.

An epistle which should begin, "My darling sweetheart and gentlemen of the jury."

A spurned woman's jilt-edged securities.

A missive calculated to speed up the males.

LOVE MAKING

Something like a good pie. All a man needs is a liberal supply of dough, applesauce, and a good spoon.

Love

LOVE NEST

A dwelling place of lovebirds that's not found in the phone book.

A place maintained by a philanderer for an exhibition of etchings.

An apartment in which a woman lives with a Cashanova.

A domicile for people who believe in affair play.

A dwelling where a female who offers no resistance hopes to lead a profitable existence.

LOVER

One to whom a pretty girl is like a malady.

A chap, about to be married, who thinks he has no bad habits.

A man who tries to be more amiable than it is possible for him to be. (*Nicholas Chamfort*)

One who vows he would die for his sweetheart or wife, but what he really means is that it is an undying love.

An unconscious comedian. (*Elbert Hubbard*)

Frequently a passing fiancé.

LOVER'S LANE

The route of all evil.

LOVE TRIANGLE

A three-sided affair that often results in a wrecktangle.

A situation where folks who are not on the square usually find themselves going around in circles.

An entanglement that calls for perfect timing of the two-timing.

PLATONIC LOVE

The gun with which the parties who are involved turns out to their surprise to be loaded.

PUPPY LOVE

One that often leads to a dog's life.

TRUE LOVE

An emotional attachment, the course of which never runs up a big light bill.

When a fellow can't help saying silly things that don't sound silly to the girl.

One that impels a woman to allow a man to keep her and then to lend him the money.

The belief that your wife looks just as good in the morning as she did in the evening.

One that enables a woman to stand a husband who eats celery audibly.

One that makes it possible for a wife to forgive her husband's failure to return her lead in bridge.

At Love's Quipping Post

There are few people who are not ashamed of their love affairs when the infatuation is over. (*La Rochefoucauld*)

Love is like war; easy to begin but very hard to stop. (*H. L. Mencken*)

Love

Men have died from time to time, but not for love. (*Shakespeare*)

Perhaps they were right in putting love into books. . . . Perhaps it could not live anywhere else. (*William Faulkner*)

The loves of some people are but the result of good suppers. (*Nicholas Chamfort*)

Some of the greatest love affairs I have even known have involved one person—unassisted. (*Wilson Mizner*)

Love matches are made by people who are content, for a month of honey, to condemn themselves to a life of vinegar. (*Countess of Blessington*)

Who marries for love without money hath merry nights and sorry days. (*John Ray*)

In the game of love, a woman who hesitates is lost, and equally so is the man who doesn't.

Love is the wisdom of the fool and the folly of the wise. (*Samuel Johnson*)

If you are not sure whether you're in love with a certain person, marry that person and you'll find out soon enough.

There is a vast difference between being constant in love and constantly in love.

Love is like a rubber band. The longer it is drawn out the thinner it gets, until eventually it breaks.

True love is like ghosts, which everybody talks about and few have seen. (*La Rochefoucauld*)

It is easier to be a lover than a husband, for the same reason that it is more difficult to be witty every day than now and then. (*Balzac*)

There are so many kisses in the world, and love gets so few of them. (*F. Andrews*)

Love is like a poached egg—appealing at first, and then when you mess around with it, it's all over the place.

The love that is fed with presents always requires feeding. (*T. L. Haines*)

The long absence is less perilous to love than the terrible trials of incessant proximity. (*Ouida*)

A man doesn't look for a happy ending to a love affair, merely one without hysterics. (from *Smart Set*)

One should always be in love. That is the reason one should never marry. (*Oscar Wilde*)

There are people who would never have fallen in love if they had never heard of love. (*La Rochefoucauld*)

Many a man in love with a dimple makes the mistake of marrying the whole girl. (*Stephen Leacock*)

To a woman the first kiss is just the end of the beginning; to a man it is the beginning of the end. (*Helen Rowland*)

People marry through a variety of other reasons, and with varying results; but to marry for love is to invite inevitable tragedy. (*James Branch Cabell*)

Love is never really understood or appreciated until it is lost.

It is a dreamy experience to be a man's first love, but it is safer to be his last.

A man is in no danger so long as he talks his love; but to write it is to impale himself on his own pothooks. (*Douglas Jerrold*)

Love

Every man has the love affair that he deserves. (*Arthur Pendenys*)

When my love swears that she is made of truth, I do believe her, though I know she lies. (*Shakespeare*)

To say that you can love one person all your life is just like saying that one candle will continue burning as long as you live. (*Tolstoy*)

The ability to make love frivolously is the chief characteristic which distinguishes human beings from beasts. (*Heywood Broun*)

When a woman feels she is in love, it is not long before she's brought to a point where she brings the man to the point.

Love is what makes you lose your head to win a hand.

Nothing in the world can compare with love as a wonderful sting.

There is no emptiness which is quite love, which strikes first in the pit of the stomach and finally winds up in the head.

Whoso loves believes the impossible. (*Proverb*)

Love enters man through his eyes, woman through her ears. (*Polish proverb*)

Love may not be altogether blind. Perhaps there are just times when it can't bear to look.

If love be good, from whence cometh my woe? (*Chaucer*)

One reason why Cupid makes so many wild shots is that he aims at the heart while looking at the legs.

In hunting and in love, you begin when you like and leave off when you can.

For only they conquer love that run away. (*Thomas Carew*)

Love is like a poker game. It starts with a pair, she gets a flush, he shows diamonds, and it ends with a full house.

Many a young man who wishes to get married because he's engaged to a peach, would be wise to leave the peach to its parent stem until he is able to preserve it.

Love is like quicksilver in the hand. Leave the fingers open and it stays in the palm; clutch it, and it darts away.

It is impossible to love and to be wise. (*Francis Bacon*)

When a couple of young people commence to eat onions, it is safe to pronounce them engaged.

Nothing is potent against love save impotence. (*Samuel Butler*)

Love is like a vaccination; when it takes, you don't have to be told.

First love is only a little foolishness and a lot of curiosity. (*George Bernard Shaw*)

Love is said to be peace, quiet, and tranquility; but that isn't love—that's sleep.

Love is the egoism of two. (*French proverb*)

Love may be blind, but a poor man is never sued for breach of promise.

Love, with women, is like the tides. Few women know the high-water mark of their love; they are always harboring the belief that it may rise still higher. (*Arnold Haultain*)

Definitions

A union between a man and a woman who start out to be good friends and subsequently change their minds.

A sweepstake in which you get a winner or tear up the ticket in the divorce court.

A wonderful institution; it's just the living together afterward that's difficult.

A feast where the grace is sometimes better than the dinner. (*Charles Caleb Colton*)

The intermission between the wedding and the divorce.

A two-handed game of solitaire.

A mutual partnership, provided both parties know when to be mute.

A triad of matrimony, acrimony, and alimony.

A sort of friendship recognized by the police. (*Robert Louis Stevenson*)

A relation that starts out as a gambol, but turns out a gamble.

A union which makes two one, and then starts a continual conflict to determine which is that one.

A miss-mating institution.

An association that makes sex legal.

A meal where the soup is better than the dessert. (*Austin O'Malley*)

A three-ring circus consisting of Engagement Ring, Wedding Ring, and Suffer-ing.

The mourning after the knot before.

An institution that it takes two people to make: a girl and her mother.

The only life sentence that is suspended by bad behavior.

A union of three kinds: trial, companionate, and fight-to-the-finish.

The alarm clock that wakes up dreaming sweethearts.

The only game of chance that the clergy favor.

The tie that blinds.

The only cure for love.

A legalized way of suppressing free speech.

The point at which a couple stop toasting, and begin roasting each other.

Marriage

A wonderful institution. It teaches you steadfastness, patience, broad-mindedness, tolerance, and a lot of other things you wouldn't need if you'd remained single.

The gateway of romance into the realm of reality.

A lottery in which men stake their liberty and women their happiness, and the only lucky gamblers are those who don't play.

A man's afterthought; a woman's all-thought.

An institution in which a man loses his bachelor's degree, and a woman gets her master's.

A period when you make progress if you just break even.

A souvenir of love. (*Helen Rowland*)

The only venture open to the cowardly. (*Voltaire*)

An institution for men and women who are afraid to think for themselves.

An institution which is popular because it combines the maximum of temptation with the maximum of opportunity. (*George Bernard Shaw*)

The way people find out what kind of mates their spouses would have preferred.

An unequalled intelligence test.

A knot tied by a preacher and untied by a lawyer.

An alliance regarded once upon a time as a contract; nowadays as a short-term option.

A long conversation chequered by disputes. (*Robert Louis Stevenson*)

An honorable agreement among men as to their conduct toward women, and it was devised by women. (*Don Herold*)

An institution that breaks up a good romance.

Quarantined love.

A union legalized by a justice of the peace of people who have neither justice nor peace thereafter.

The hangover from the intoxication of passion.

An institution in which couples constantly face the music, beginning with "Here Comes the Bride."

A word which should be pronounced "mirage." (*Herbert Spencer*)

An alliance that some men and women enter into with open minds—holes in the head.

A ghastly public confession of a strictly private intention. (*Ian Hay*)

A union which begins when a man meets the only woman with understands him, and ends with a divorce for the same reason.

What a man gets when all he's really looking for is a disengagement.

The institution which guarantees that one's troubles will be over—many things.

The Sphinx-riddle. Solve it, or be torn to bits, is the decree. (*D. H. Lawrence*)

An institution that may be made in heaven, but is getting some gosh-awful maintenance work on earth.

Marriage

An alliance regarded by husbands as a womanacle and by wives as a labor union.

The thing that men and women enter into because they don't know what to do with themselves, or haven't a thing in the world to worry about.

A lottery in which the wife sometimes loses—she does not always become a widow.

An institution consisting of three stages: hooked, booked, cooked.

An end of many short follies—being one long stupidity. (*Nietzsche*)

A union in which the most dangerous year is the first, then the second, third, fourth, fifth, etc., etc., etc.

A community consisting of a master, a mistress, and two slaves—making in all two. (*Ambrose Bierce*)

The world's best-known fire-extinguisher.

The wedded state, where the vows that were taken were easier said than done.

An institution that men and women enter into for better or for wars.

A snore and a delusion.

A condition that a woman aspires to and a man submits to.

A 50-50 proposition; but unfortunately too many couples do not understand fractions.

The only union which permits a woman to work unlimited overtime without extra pay.

The state of matrimony that's bad if it's solely a matter-o'-money.

The thing that's difficult to keep square with a triangle.

The only quiz show in which you lose if you give the correct answer.

A situation where two metals have been welded with the temper unremoved.

A ceremony in which the ring is put on the finger of the lady and through the nose of the gentleman. (*Herbert Spencer*)

A woman's hair net tangled in a man's spectacles on top of the bedroom dresser. (*Don Herold*)

The foreclosure of the mortgage on the future happiness of a person who has an undesirable mate.

Putting one's hand into a bag of snakes on the chance of drawing out an eel. (*Leonardo da Vinci*)

An arrangement that begins as a duet and turns into a duel.

A thing that often happens when a man gets hooked with his own line.

A sacrament by virtue of which each imparts nothing but vexations to the other. (*Balzac*)

The matrimonial high sea, for which a compass has yet to be invented.

Something like an artichoke; you have to go through so much to get so little.

A besieged fortress; those without want to get in, and those who are in want to get out.

Marriage

A many-spending thing following courtship—the many-splendid thing.

A device originated by females for looting the males.

A romantic story that begins by a splashing waterfall and ends up over a leaky kitchen faucet.

An institution for love. Since love is blind, it is understandable why marriage is referred to as an institution for the blind.

The union folks are prone to join while they are laboring under a delusion.

A romance in which the hero or, as the case may be, the heroine dies in the first chapter.

A thing like a boxing event. The preliminaries are frequently better than the main event.

A lottery in which the prize winner draws alimony.

When a man gets billed for the time he cooed.

A book of which the first chapter is written in poetry and the remaining chapters in prose. (*Beverly Nichols*)

The portal through which rapturous lovers return from paradise to earth.

Something like the measles; we all have to go through it. (*Jerome K. Jerome*)

Something like a warm bath; once you get used to it, it's not so hot.

Something like shopping in a department store. It's all over when you buy.

Where a man takes a wife to take care of him so that she can make him strong enough for her to lean on.

The interim period between courtship and divorce.

A state of martyrdom assumed by men and women for a period of time to prepare them for a better world.

An institution that frightens a lot of unmarried people—and a lot of married people too.

Proof that two can live as bitter as one.

A union that often makes estranged bedfellows.

An institution which countless people do not regard as a lottery; in a lottery you can win once in a while.

An alliance into which some people enter for love, some for money, but far too many for a short time.

A repast in the Chinese style, starting with the sweetmeat and ending in the soup. (*Ethel Watts Mumford*)

A time-honored institution that's almost like being in love.

MARRIAGEABLE AGE

Any time between the seminary and the cemetery.

MARRIAGE CEREMONY

Going to the halter.

One that takes an hour more or less, but its troubles last a lifetime.

MARRIAGE CRACK-UP

One that often occurs when the installment collector cracks down.

Marriage

MARRIAGE KNOT

One that is sometimes tied so tightly that it wounds those whom it unites. (*Burgnot de Varennes*)

MARRIAGE LAWS

Along with police, armies and navies, the mark of human incompetence. (*Mrs. Bertrand Russell*)

MARRIAGE LICENSE

A hunting permit that entitles you to one dear at a time.

A formal permission to join in wedlock that is often spelled "mirage" license.

A noosepaper.

An IOU for all the rash promises people make when they're courting.

MARRIAGE PROPOSAL

An impulsive speech frequently made on the purr of the moment.

Something a woman can listen to faster than a man can talk.

MARRIAGE RITUAL

An observance of set wedding ceremonial forms that are easier said than done.

MARRIAGE TIES

A misnomer. In an argument, the wife always wins.

Frequently only slipknots.

MARRIAGE VOW

The solemn promise that would be more accurate if declared, "Until debt do us part."

One that young marrying couples appear to have taken to mean "Love, Honor, and no Baby."

MATRIMONIAL BARK

One that is often wrecked by matrimonial barking.

MATRIMONIAL BONDS

Obligations that are worthless unless the interest is kept up.

MATRIMONIAL FLARE-UP

One that if often caused by an old flame.

MATRIMONIAL SEA

A phrase that owes its designation to the fact that so many couples find it difficult to keep their heads above water.

One that starts with a wave of enthusiasm that does not always remain a permanent wave.

One that must be real rough, judging by the way married couples sail into each other.

Kinds of Marriage

BEEF-STEW MARRIAGE

One where the wife is always beefing and the husband is always stewed.

COMMON-LAW MARRIAGE

A couple living in unholy bedlock.

When a woman mates a man halfway.

Marriage

DICTIONARY MARRIAGE

One where one word leads to another.

HAPPY MARRIAGE

One in which a couple are sure to have three essential books—Prayer book, checkbook, and cookbook.

HARMONIOUS MARRIAGE

One that produces sweet music when one of the parties is satisfied to play second fiddle.

IDEAL MARRIAGE

A union in which the parties are as polite to each other as if they were just friends.

LASTING MARRIAGE

One in which the husband likes his wife better than he likes anyone else's.

Welded bliss.

One where both parties have better mates than they deserve.

MODERN MARRIAGE

One in which any similarity to a couple's perfect understanding and willingness to compromise is strictly frictional.

Where the wife keeps everything but her husband.

NIP-AND-TUCK MARRIAGE

One where the husband is always taking a nip, and the wife has to tuck him in.

SECOND MARRIAGE

The triumph of hope over experience.

One which may give a person a new leash or louse on life.

UNHAPPY MARRIAGE

One in which the parties haven't learned to get along without things which they have no right to expect anyway.

One where the parties have stopped dating and have started intimidating.

One where a couple would be ashamed to sell their family parrot to the town gossip.

At the Matrimonial Quipping Post

The difference is wide that the bedsheets will not decide. (*Proverb*)

A woman worries about the future until she gets a husband. A man never worries about the future until he gets a wife.

Though thou canst not forebear to love, forebear to link. (*Sir Walter Raleigh*)

If they only married when they fell in love, most people would die unwed. (*Robert Louis Stevenson*)

It is claimed by marriage counselors that a little common sense would prevent divorces. A little common sense would prevent lot of marriages.

Marriage is a covered dish. (*Proverb*)

When couples lament that the magic has gone out of their marriage, it may be that they have caught on to each other's tricks.

While the chief effect of love may be to drive one or both of the parties half crazy, it is unfortunate that the chief effect of marriage is that it so often finishes the job.

Marriage

It isn't tying himself to one woman that a man dreads when he thinks of marriage; it's separating himself from all the others. (*Helen Rowland*)

They dream in courtship, but in wedlock wake. (*Alexander Pope*)

There must be lots of good in most married folks—because so little of it comes out.

Too many couples follow the path of least assistance.

When a woman marries again, it is because she detested her first husband; when a man marries again, it is because he adores his first wife. (*Oscar Wilde*)

The trouble with marriage is not with the institution. It's the personnel.

In matters of religion and matrimony I never give advice; because I will not have anybody's torments in this world or the next laid to my charge. (*Lord Chesterfield*)

Lots of married folks have never thought of divorce, but of murder—plenty.

Many people's idea of a happy marriage is the next one.

Chief among men and women who are bound to go far are those seeking an ideal mate.

Often and often, a marriage hardly differs from prostitution, except being hard to escape from. (*Bertrand Russell*)

Marriage is like life in this—that it is a field of battle, not a bed of roses. (*Robert Louis Stevenson*)

A woman accepts a man for the sake of marriage, whereas a man accepts marriage for the sake of a woman.

The one charm of marriage is that it makes a life of deception absolutely necessary for both parties. (*Oscar Wilde*)

The one thing that often brings a couple together is the dress that has to be buttoned up in the back.

It's not always the vices that married people can't bear in one another; it's their virtues, carried to excess, that can become unbearable.

People say you musn't love your friend's wife, but how are you to love your enemy's wife? (*George Moore*)

Marriage is like eating in a restaurant. After you've ordered, you notice what someone else has, and you wish you had taken that.

Marriage is like twirling a baton, turning handsprings, or eating with chopsticks; it looks so easy till you try it. (*Helen Rowland*)

Don't marry an entire family, or it may work out that way. (*George Ade*)

Many people are unhappily married, but fortunately they don't know it.

What nonsense people talk about happy marriages. A man can be happy so long as he doesn't love her. (*George Bernard Shaw*)

In the opinion of many married people, "altar" is a term which must have been invented by an Englishman who dropped his *h*'s.

I'll marry anyone you like on one condition; her wedding tomorrow, and her wake the day after. (*Plautus*, 210 B.C.)

Marriage

Oh! How many torments lie in the small circle of a wedding ring. (*Balzac*)

I am to be married within these three days—married past redemption. (*John Dryden*)

Marriage may be called many things, but in the opinion of many married people it's anything but a joke. They're still trying to get a laugh out of it.

On record are innumerable cases of husbands and wives who were ecstatically happy for many years—and then they met.

Who marries does well; who marries not, does better. (*Proverb*)

Wedding rings are much lighter and thinner nowadays. In the memory of old-timers, they were meant to last a lifetime.

Where incompatibility is given as grounds for divorce, the trouble may frequently be found in the first two syllables.

Many an unhappy marriage may be found among grammatically correct couples—where wives say "You shall" and husbands say "I will."

No married household can hang out the sign, "Nothing's the matter here." (*Chinese proverb*)

The shortest marriage bedtime story: *"Move over!"*

The only time some married couples' minds seem to be running in the same channel is when they're watching TV.

One advantage of marriage is that you can't do something stupid without hearing about it.

Bachelors know more about women than married men; if they didn't, they'd be married too. (*H. L. Mencken*)

It does not much signify whom one marries, as one is sure to find out next morning that it is someone else. (*Samuel Rogers*)

They say a parson first invented gunpowder, but one cannot believe it until one is married. (*Douglas Jerrold*)

If you are afraid of loneliness, do not marry. (*Anton Chekhov*)

Behind every successful man stands a woman—his wife or his mother-in-law, telling him how stupid he is.

When people say they're satisfied with married life, they probably mean they've had just about all they want of it.

Do you think your mother and I should have lived so comfortably together if ever we had been married? (*John Gay*)

What they do in heaven we are ignorant of; but what they do not do we are told expressly, they neither marry nor are given in marriage. (*Jonathan Swift*)

Society would be delightful were all women married and all men single. (*Edgar Saltus*)

Folks who get married to have someone to tell their troubles to often find that they have plenty to talk about.

It is becoming increasingly clear that people wouldn't be getting divorced for such foolish, flimsy reasons if they didn't get married for such foolish, flimsy reasons.

Think of your ancestors and your posterity, and you will never marry. (*Ethel Watts Mumford*)

Marriage

Married life hasn't changed in two thousand years. Greek wives used to sit up to 3:00 A.M. to listen to a lyre too.

The honeymoon is over when a mate's idiosyncrasies become faults.

The honeymoon is over when he gets out of the car at a drive-in movie to wipe off the windshield.

The honeymoon is over when he phones that he'll be late for dinner, and she's already left a note that it's in the refrigerator.

Whenever a husband and wife begin to discuss their marriage, they are giving evidence at an inquest. (*H. L. Mencken*)

Whoever first said that a husband and wife are one never heard the two quarreling.

More things belong to marriage than four bare legs in a bed. (*John Heywood*)

The chief reason why marriage is rarely a success is that it is contracted while the partners are insane. (*John Collins*)

Men marry because they are tired; women because they are curious. Both are disappointed. (*Oscar Wilde*)

The last time some married people did everything together was getting married the same day.

Successful marriages must not only be based on the cookbook and the checkbook, but on the Good Book.

It's impossible for a woman to be married to the same man for any long period of time. In just a short time, he's not the same man.

There's one thing many couples agree on—that they never should have married in the first place.

After a few years of marriage, a man can look right at a woman without seeing her, and she can see right through him without looking at him. (*Helen Rowland*)

When a husband and wife see eye to eye, they're probably the same height.

Some people are investment-conscious, except concerning the bonds of matrimony—where the interest lags.

For a marriage to really be successful, friendship must supplement love.

It must be true that marriage is made in Heaven. It certainly needs an unearthly amount of tolerance and compromise.

A little incompatibility is the spice of life, particularly if he has income and she is pattable. (*George Ade*)

Behind every successful married man stand four people—his wife, his mother-in-law, and Mr. and Mrs. Jones.

The happiest marriages are those in which a man can make his wife do anything she wants to do.

The man who enters his wife's dressing room is either a philosopher or a fool. (*Balzac*)

The trouble with marriage is that, while every woman is at heart a mother, every man is at heart a bachelor. (*Edward V. Lucas*)

If husbands and wives are really one, how come it takes two to make a quarrel?

When a man says he's sure of his wife, it simply means he's sure of her; but when she's sure of him, it means she's sure of herself.

Marriage

Lots of folks who are married for the second time now lament that they didn't deserve to lose their first mates.

Many married people think they're well mated until the TV set breaks down, and they suddenly have an opportunity for conversation.

The Constitution guarantees only the *pursuit* of happiness —not happiness itself; that's up to the married couples themselves.

The thing that puzzles married people most is how the Joneses do it on their salaries.

The lottery business is rapidly being ruined by the rumor that marriage is a lottery.

The ideal marriage would seem to be the one where the wife is a treasure and the husband a treasury.

Marriage is the only known business in which a man takes his boss along on his vacation.

Some of the unhappiest married people may be found among those whose first mates divorced them and whose second mates won't.

Gifts that are exchanged by married people may not replace true love, but they do have a way of easing the trials of marriage.

The same conditions should be made in marriage as in the case of short-term house rentals, with the option of becoming the purchaser if the house suits. (*Prince de Ligne*)

The marriage system created a new sport—adultery. (*Holbrook Jackson*)

There's nothing some men wouldn't do for their wives, and there's nothing their wives wouldn't do for them; in fact, they go throughout their entire lives doing nothing for each other.

Statistics reveal that the number of wives taken on business trips is considerably larger than the number of marriage licenses that have been issued.

The home circle can never be kept square with a triangle.

A lot of married folks who claim they only tell white lies are undoubtedly color-blind.

It's getting to a point where people never know just what they're going to do from one husband or wife to another.

Storm Warnings

Strange to say what delight we married people have to see these poor fools decoyed into our condition. (*Samuel Pepys*)

Advice to persons about to be married. Don't! (*Henry Mayhew* in *Punch*)

Nothing is better than a single life. (*Horace*)

The music at a marriage procession always reminds me of the music of soldiers marching to battle. (*Heinrich Heine*)

Man and wife make one fool. (*Ben Jonson*)

Before going to war say a prayer; before going to sea say two prayers; before marrying say three prayers. (*Proverb*)

Marriage is a bargain, and somebody has to get the worst of the bargain. (*Helen Rowland*)

Marriage

If marriages are made in heaven, you have but few friends there. (*Proverb*)

Many a good hanging prevents a bad marriage. (*Shakespeare*)

Wedded persons may thus pass over their lives quietly if the husband becomes deaf and the wife blind. (*Richard Taverner*)

Marriage is a very sea of calls and claims, which have but little to do with love. (*Henrik Ibsen*)

A man and woman marry because both of them do not know what to do with themselves. (*Chekhov*)

Marriage is neither heaven nor hell; it is simply purgatory. (*Abraham Lincoln*)

Love in marriage would be the realization of a beautiful dream, if marriage were not too often the end of it. (*Alphonse Karr*)

Though women are angels, yet wedlock's the devil. (*Byron*)

I never married, and I wish my father never had. (*Greek proverb*)

There are some good marriages, but practically no delightful ones. (*La Rochefoucauld*)

Marriage in our days? I would almost say it is a rape by contract. (*Michelet*)

'Tis my maxim, he's a fool that marries; but he's a greater fool that does not marry a fool. (*William Wycherly*)

3 HUSBANDS vs. WIVES

Definitions

A husband is . . .

A man who made the wrong turn in Lover's Lane.

One who may not be the best-informed man, but positively is the most-informed.

An Argus abroad, a mole at home.

A man who gave up privileges he never knew he had.

A bachelor who didn't notice when a woman closed the escape hatch.

The average between what one woman thinks she got and another woman thinks she missed.

Husbands vs. Wives

One who is admonished by the minister at his wedding: "Remember! Of the unspoken word, thou art master."

A man of conviction—after he knows what his wife thinks.

One who is married to a woman who complains she has nothing to wear, and needs four closets to keep it in.

The consummation of a woman's spousing project.

One whose wife knows his jokes backwards—and tells them that way.

A man who did not take advantage of the fact that marriage is not compulsory.

One whose wife loves him so much, he can make her do anything she wants to do.

A rake whose wife has turned him into a lawn mower.

A man who embarked on the good ship Matrimony as the skipper, only to learn soon that he's the second mate.

What's left of a sweetheart after the nerve has been killed.

A bachelor whose luck finally failed him.

A night owl who has been turned into a homing pigeon.

One who can always tell what kind of a time he's having at a party by the look on his wife's face.

A man who is a big shot in his home—until the company leaves.

A domesticated animal capable of being skinned more than once.

One for whom before marriage it was wine, woman, and song; now it's beer, mama, and TV.

A man who grows old all alone; after a certain age his wife has stopped having birthdays.

A person who can always tell when his wife has taken out the car—by the tracks across the lawn.

One who never realizes how little he knows until he tells his wife how to run the house.

A fellow who has two chances of winning an argument with his wife—slim and none.

A chap who regrets that he didn't falter at the altar.

A man who can say anything he pleases in his own home—his wife and children never listen anyway.

A man who swore his love by the stars and has now come down to earth.

A person who has two sides: the side his wife knows, and the side he foolishly thinks she doesn't know.

One who is the head of the family; but his wife is the neck, and whichever way she turns, he goes.

A chap who got married because the girl was as pretty as a melody—and now he's facing the music.

One who always meets a marital crisis with a firm hand—full of peace offerings.

One who never knows when he's well off because he never is.

A man who can always manage to keep a couple of jumps ahead of his wife—if he plays checkers with her.

A person who knows how to stop that noise in his car—he lets his wife drive.

Husbands vs. Wives

One who now knows it would have been better if he had let himself be laughed at for being unmarried, than not to be able to laugh because he is.

A man who definitely knows how a wife should be managed, but somehow never seems to be able to act on the knowledge.

One who knows the best time to take out the garbage—when his wife tells him to.

A man who can never pull the wool over his wife's eyes with the wrong yarn.

An old-fashioned individual who expects his wife to help him with the dishes.

One who could lead a nice life if his wife would only let him do a little leading.

One who doesn't believe the statistics that married men live longer than single men; he claims it only seems longer.

The victim of the only known sport in which the animal that gets caught has to buy the license.

A man who was crazy to get married—but didn't realize it at the time.

Matrimony's silent partner.

A man of few words.

A peaceful individual who loves his wife still.

One who blames his troubles on Adam for not having been Adam-ant.

A man who has given the best ears of his life to his wife.

A person who's happy when his wife is in bed, safe and soundless.

A man who doesn't hesitate to lay down the law to his wife —but promptly accepts all her amendments.

A fellow who may not appear to be against marriage as much as he is up against it.

One who feels it's best to tell his wife everything—before someone else does.

A man who answers dutifully to his wife's four requirements for a good husband—cash, stocks, bonds, and credit cards.

One who gives his wife the best expense-account years of his life.

A fellow whose wife has changed very much since he married her—his friends, his habits, and his hours.

One who married a willowy woman, only to find her weeping-willowy.

A man whose wife isn't as concerned about outer space as she is about closet space.

One who knows that American wives are the best-yessed women anywhere.

One who boasts that he runs the show in his home, but neglects to mention that his wife writes the script.

A man who has learned that keeping a secret from a married woman is like sneaking daybreak past a rooster.

A person who wonders why if a woman's intuition is so good she always has to ask questions.

Husbands vs. Wives

A misguided individual who thinks that his wife thinks that he is the boss.

A man who stood at the altar with a smile on his face, oblivious to the fact that he was so young to go.

One who wishes that his wife would be more interested in mending his socks than his ways.

A chap who knows that his wife is never happier than when he is poking funds at her.

One who never ceases to wonder how a married woman can keep breaking things—like 10's, 20's and 50's.

One who has discovered that women enjoy matrimony because it is a state that has a governor.

A person who has to keep his earning capacity up to his wife's yearning capacity.

A man who calls his wife an angel because she's always harping on things, always flitting about, and always saying she has nothing to wear.

One who thinks nothing is too good for his wife—and so does she.

One who works hard to keep his wife in the mink of condition.

A man who is aware of his wife's keen sense of humor—the more she's humored, the better she likes it.

What happens to a man because some woman wasn't keen on being an old maid.

The man who came, saw, and concurred.

One who lives in a man's world, but it's in his wife's name.

A fellow who exchanged a bushel of fun for a peck of trouble.

Familiar Types

AGREEABLE HUSBAND
One who is always agreeing with his wife.

CHECKMATED HUSBAND
One who allows his wife to write the checks.

DEAD HUSBAND
One who was so busy making money for an abundant life that he ended up leaving an abundant wife.

DELIRIOUS HUSBAND
A may lying ill in the hospital who keeps calling for his wife.

DIPLOMATIC HUSBAND
One who remembers his wife's birthday, but forgets which one it is.

DISILLUSIONED HUSBAND
A man who married a woman for her looks, but not the kind he's getting now.

FAITHFUL HUSBAND
One who sends his alimony checks on time.

FIRST HUSBAND
One who is mourned by his wife's sorrow-stricken second husband.

Husbands vs. Wives

GOOD HUSBAND

A man who feels in his pockets every time he passes a mailbox.

LINGUISTIC HUSBAND

One who has the ability to speak several languages and keep his mouth shut in one.

MODEL HUSBAND

Any other woman's.

One who is all right if he's a working model with a good income.

OVERWORKING HUSBAND

One whose senseless whirl can be described in three words—Hurry, Worry, Bury.

RICH HUSBAND

One who owes his financial success to his curiosity to find out if there was any income his wife couldn't live beyond.

SMART HUSBAND

One who lets his wife think she has her own way—and then lets her have it.

One who gets along by staying on listening terms with his wife.

STRONG-WILLED HUSBAND

One who is definitely not a yes-man. When his wife say No, he says No.

TENDER HUSBAND

One who is kept in hot water all the time.

Wives (of a Sort)

BLONDE WIFE

An established bleachhead.

COLD WIFE

One who has been refused a fur coat.

CONSIDERATE WIFE

A housewife who sometimes threads the needle for her husband when he goes to sew his buttons on his shirts.

One who always forgives her husband when she is in the wrong.

One who has set aside a special room for her husband where he can smoke his cigars to his heart's content—the garage.

COOPERATIVE WIFE

A woman who tries to help her husband solve all the complicated problems which would never have arisen if he hadn't married her.

ECONOMICAL WIFE

A woman who doesn't need to hire domestic help—she married it.

One who uses 35 candles on her 40th birthday.

EXPECTING WIFE

One who is expecting a new country home, a new car, a new mink coat, et cetera.

Husbands vs. Wives

FAITHLESS WIFE

A spicy dish who thinks she needs more pepper.

One who is more interested in spice than spouse.

A home-loving woman. When her husband is away she is home, loving another man.

One who every once in a while feels like a new man.

One who gets indifferent—in different men's arms.

A woman whose husband's absence makes her heart go wander.

FRETFUL WIFE

A woman who broadcasts over a fretwork of wrinkles.

A woman who whines her husband around her little finger.

FRIGID WIFE

One who has gender but not sex.

A married woman whose kisses are electric—like an electric refrigerator, that is.

One who doesn't realize that what is more desirable than an attractive wife to behold is one to be held.

FUSSY WIFE

One who is so neat that if her husband gets up during the night for a drink of water, the bed is made when he gets back.

A bustling housewife who empties the ash trays even before they're used.

One who even irons shoelaces.

GOOD-HEARTED WIFE

A woman who hits her hubby with the soft end of the mop.

HENPECKING WIFE

One who is enough to make a husband she-sick.

A woman with a whim of iron.

One who hangs towels in the bathroom marked Hers and Stupid's.

The marriage partner of a man with a lot of irons in the fire—she keeps burning his golf clubs.

A female Tartar who even complains about the noise her husband is making when he's fixing his own breakfast.

A vixen who wakes her husband up from his sound sleep if she sees a smile on his face.

One whose husband always throws his arms around her when he comes into the house—sometimes before she can even strike a blow.

A woman who, when she runs her fingers through her husband's hair, is after his scalp.

One whose husband frequently phones home to say he left his lunch money in his apron pocket.

A woman whose husband, from the time he said "I do," hasn't been able to say another word.

One who jumps whenever her husband speaks—all over him.

A mate with a simple arrangement for the avoidance of arguments. Half the time she does what she wants, and half the time he does what she wants.

Husbands vs. Wives

A womanager who thinks she has been given the legal right of suppressing free speech.

One whose husband has gone from a bachelor apartment to a doghouse.

A woman who got married in order to have a home in order to have a husband to order.

One in whose house there's no need for dishes; her husband eats out of her hand.

A married woman who can be read like a book, but can't be shut up like one.

One whose husband washes up when asked, and dries up when told.

One who likes a home that's based on law and order, as long as she can lay down the law and give the order.

A wisp of a woman with a will-o'-the-wisp.

A man's bitter half.

The hen that crows in an unhappy house where the cock holds his peace.

One who lives both her life and her husband's, and doesn't do so well with his.

The marriage partner of a man of few words.

One whose husband never knows when he's well off, because he never is.

A mate who doesn't have to raise the roof. All she has to do is raise an eyebrow.

A she-wolf with a busband who is her altered ego.

One whose husband wears the pants in the family—under the apron.

A woman whose husband not only can't express an opinion, but even has to wipe it off his face.

One who likes her husband to worship the ground she gives him the run-around on.

One who has turned a man-about-town into a mouse-around the house.

One whose husband thinks twice before saying nothing.

The woman of the house in which there are differences of opinion—but her husband makes sure she doesn't know it.

One who the instant her husband complains the coffee is cold makes it hot for him.

IDEAL WIFE

A beautiful, wealthy, passionate deaf-mute who owns a distillery.

JEALOUS WIFE

One who envies Eve, who, if she suspected Adam of infidelity could count his ribs.

LAZY WIFE

A married woman who thinks her works was done when she swept down the aisle.

A housewife for whose husband life is one undarned thing after another.

A housekeeper who sweeps the room with a glance.

One whose act of putting her finger through the wedding ring was the last thing she did by hand.

Husbands vs. Wives

One who has kept her promise to keep the kitchen spotless —they eat out.

MAGNETIC WIFE

Everything she wears is charged.

MODERN WIFE

Liberty Belle.

One who does her preserving in front of a mirror instead of the kitchen stove.

A woman without fear—except of a stack of dishes.

One whose chief forms of exercise seem to be running up bills and jumping to conclusions.

A person who can dish it out, but can't cook it.

One whose cooking often brings a lump to her husband's throat that only baking soda can remove.

A woman who tells her husband she has a marvelous meal planned for him, and tells him all about it on the way to the restaurant.

One who likes her husband to be a salesman because he is used to taking orders.

A woman who seems to believe that the marriage vow was "to love, honor, and display."

NARROW-MINDED WIFE

One whose narrow waist and broad mind have swapped places.

OFT-MARRIED WIFE

A woman who has some of her towels monogrammed *HERS* and *TO WHOM IT MAY CONCERN* and others, *HIS, HERS,* and *NEXT.*

One who has led several men to the halter.

OLD-FASHIONED WIFE

One who could remember her husband's first kiss; as distinguished from the modern wife who can hardly remember her first husband.

The old-fashioned wife vowed to "Love, honor and obey until death do us part." The modern wife vows to "Love, honor and display until debt do us part."

The old-fashioned wife saved her wedding dress for sentimental reasons. The modern wife saves her wedding dress for her next wedding.

The old-fashioned wife made her husband feel like a new man, The modern wife drops her husband when she feels like a new man.

The old-fashioned wife learned to cook to find a way into her husband's heart. The modern wife thaw an easier way.

The old-fashioned wife's greatest danger in the kitchen was burns. The modern wife's greatest danger is frostbite.

The old-fashioned wife darned her husband's socks. The modern wife socks her darned husband.

OVERWEIGHT WIFE

A bulge in a girdled cage.

One whose dangerous curves have become extended detours.

Husbands vs. Wives

A woman who fails to practice girth control.

One whose figure has gone to waist strictly of her own chewsing.

A woman who isn't sylph-conscious.

PRETTY WIFE

One who looks as pretty as when you married her—but it takes her a little longer now.

SCHIZOPHRENIC WIFE

A mate with a split personality. Her towels are embroidered HERS and HERS.

SPENDTHRIFT WIFE

A fund-loving mate.

One who loves her husband for all he's worth.

A woman who believes in giving her husband all the credit she can get.

One whose husband isn't worried about the purchasing power of the dollar. He's more worried about her purchasing power.

A dame who got married to have someone to spend with the rest of her life.

One who raises her standard of living by lowering her husband's resistance.

A woman whose chief interest is the purse. She even purses her lips when her husband kisses her.

One of whom it can truly be said, "What a woman!" Without her, her husband would never be what he is today—broke.

A female whose ship of matrimony would move more smoothly—so far as her husband is concerned—if she stayed away from the sales.

An extremely punctual lady—everything she buys is on time.

One who starts walking when her husband's money stops talking.

A woman who is the perfect exemplification of the law of supply and demand. She demands and her husband supplies.

One whose husband's only voice in their marital affairs is the invoice.

A mate who, when she asks for pin money, means one with twenty diamonds in it.

A woman who claims her husband owes everything to her and, boy, she sure is collecting!

An expensive woman with a pensive husband.

A woman who can be very nice when she wants—and she wants plenty.

A man's getter half.

One who is less interested in the cookbook than in the checkbook.

A woman who knows how to make a dollar go far—so far that her husband never sees it again.

A female who spends to keep looking stunning, while her husband looks stunned.

One who thinks that the marriage vow was "To love and cherish, until debt do us part."

One whose upkeep may be her husband's downfall.

Husbands vs. Wives

A marriage partner to whom all that matters is the present.

A married woman who is willing to put up with shackles so long as there are shekels.

One who can get jewelry and furs without half crying.

One who likes to be part of a balanced couple—where hubby makes the money and she spends it.

A woman who believes her husband should follow the government's example and raise the debt ceiling.

SUBMISSIVE WIFE

One who submits to her husband when he tells her to do as she pleases.

TALKATIVE WIFE

An oft-spoken married woman.

A husband's source of earitation.

One whose children carry a picture of their father, and a sound track of her.

A thing of beauty and a jaw forever.

A married woman with no minor voices.

A woman who is sure to win an argument with her husband, because words flail him.

Matrimony's vocalamity.

The Trouble with Wives

Wives are usually their husbands' mental inferiors and spiritual superiors; this gives them double instruments of torture. (*Don Herold*)

There are several ways to handle a wife, but unfortunately men have never discovered what they are.

No one knows better than a husband why they say charity begins at home; that's were poverty starts.

Being married to a sleepy-souled woman is just like playing cards for nothing; no passion is excited, and the time is filled up. (*Samuel Johnson*)

A lot of men who wondered before marriage how a man could live without a woman know the answer now—cheaper.

Every woman is wrong until she cries, and then she is right, instantly. (*Thomas Chandler Haliburton*)

The way to fight a woman is with your hat—grab it and run. (*John Barrymore*)

Although both husbands and wives now wear pants, it's easy to tell one from the other. The one that's listening is the husband.

Married men have one advantage over bachelors. There's something tranquilizing about knowing the worst.

The mechanical lie detector will never be as effective as the one made from Adam's rib.

Any man can acquire a large vocabulary—he can marry it.

Whenever you see a want ad for a mature woman, you can be sure it was inserted by the boss's wife.

A man is in general better pleased when he has a good dinner upon his table than when his wife talks Greek. (*Samuel Johnson*)

Husbands vs. Wives

Statistics show that there are more men than women in mental institutions. Husbands aver that it just goes to show who's driving who crazy.

The saddest thing about a woman with a mind of her own is her husband.

Many a man is in bad shape because he married a woman primarily because she was in good shape.

Everybody all over the world takes a wife's estimate into account in forming an opinion of a man. (*Balzac*)

Wives would do well to realize that the best way to protect a wedding ring is to dip it in dishwater a couple of times a day.

In choosing a wife, a man should bear the old proverb in mind: "A daughter is as the mother was."

Marrying a girl for her looks only is like buying a house just because of the paint job.

It is better to marry a quiet fool than a witty scold. (*Proverb*)

In these modern times, a man has no right to complain of having made a mistake in choosing a wife—he certainly sees what he's getting.

American women expect to find in their husbands a perfection that English women only hope to find in their butlers. (*W. Somerset Maugham*)

A man is foolish to worry about things beyond his control—like his wife, for instance.

A husband doesn't mind his wife's ability to read him like a book. What he objects to is that instead of skipping what she doesn't like, she goes over and over it.

The quickest way for a husband to dry his wifes' tears is to throw in the sponge.

The fellow who dates a different woman every week may be doing so because he sleeps with an indifferent wife every night.

No wife can endure a gambling husband—unless he's a steady winner. (*Thomas Dewar*)

The mechanical lie detector will never be as effective or successful as the one made from Adam's rib.

In marriage, for a man, in order to get the precise thing or things that he wants, he has to take a lot of other things that he does not want. (*H. L. Mencken*)

Sad but true that some wives draw the very highest wages for unskilled labor.

Many a woman would make a better wife if she weren't so busy trying to make a better husband.

It's truly remarkable how intuitive some wives are. They're able to contradict their husbands even before they say anything on a subject.

A husband always knows what is the matter with his wife, for she always knows what is not. (*Balzac*)

In any argument with his wife, a man cannot understand why women are called the fair sex.

One day husbands will get together and petition Congress for a higher tax on bachelors. It isn't fair that some men should be happier than others.

Famous last words: "No woman is going to tell me what to do."

Husbands vs. Wives

Going to an out-of-town convention with your wife is like going fishing with a game warden.

Not all men who leave their wives are deserters—some are refugees.

Everything in life is fairly simple—except one's wife. (*Don Herold*)

It's a funny thing that when a man hasn't anything on earth to worry about, he goes off and gets married. (*Robert Frost*)

Strange how a girl who walks on air when she gets engaged just can't wait until after the wedding to put her foot down.

The man who claims he's the boss in his home is either bragging or has a wife who never stays home.

If he has a quarrel with his wife, the modern husband goes to his club. Maybe the primitive husband had a better idea—he reached for it.

If men knew how woman pass the time when they're alone, they'd never marry. (*O. Henry*)

A husband can discourage his wife from buying that new hat she's trying on, by saying: "Of course you can buy it, dear. I like that middle-aged look it gives you."

Behind every woman with expensive jewelry and a chinchilla coat is a husband who once swore she'd never get them.

The cynical husband is certain of the chief reason why women live longer than men—women don't have wives to live with.

It's better to have courage than a wife. A man can't have both. (*Life*)

The man who is unhappy because he hasn't found a perfect woman whom he can marry will be far unhappier if he ever finds her.

Some men are born meek, get married, and then have to stay that way.

After all is said and done, it's usually the wife who has said it and the husband who has done it.

Married men live longer than single men; at least, they complain more about it. (*Don Herold*)

All men are created equal. If they get married, it's their own fault.

There is no such thing as a dangerous woman; there are only susceptible men. (*Joseph Wood Krutch*)

Wives are no longer propagandizing for equal rights with husbands. It would be quite a comedown for them.

The man who backs down when he's wrong is wise. The man who gives in when he's wrong is married.

Many a man might become a bigamist if it weren't for the awesome prospect of two mothers-in-law.

The Bible says that the last thing God made was woman; He must have made her on a Saturday night—it shows fatigue. (*Dumas, pére*)

A man who desires to get married should know everything or nothing. (*George Bernard Shaw*)

There are any number of men who say they are the boss in their own homes. They lie about other things too.

By all means marry; if you get a good wife, you'll become happy; if you get a bad one, you'll become a philosopher. (*Socrates*)

Husbands vs. Wives

Some women henpeck their husbands and then wonder why he's listening to some other chick.

Women are outliving men by an average of five years. Husbands say it's because women don't have wives to live with.

A survey discloses that married men are more inventive than single men. What's so unusual about that? They have to be.

The smart husband lets his wife know right from the start who's the boss. He knows there's no use deluding himself.

Well-educated women have an advantage as wives. They have a better vocabulary for explaining why they are such poor housekeepers.

Only choose in marriage a woman whom you would choose as a friend if she were a man. (*Joubert*)

He knows little who tells his wife all he knows. (*Thomas Fuller*)

A man may be a fool and not know it—but not if he is married. (*H. L. Mencken*)

The clever wife knows that her best hobby is the one that interests the man she's interested in.

When a woman loves her husband, he can make her do anything she wants to do.

In certain parts of Asia a man doesn't know his wife until he marries her. But why single out Asia?

Most wives are nicer than their husbands, but that's nothing; I am nice to everybody from whom I can get money. (*Don Herold*)

A woman complains that when her husband sees an attractive girl he forgets he's a married man; but that's exactly when he remembers.

The only way a woman can ever reform her husband is by boring him so completely that he loses all possible interest in life. (*Oscar Wilde*)

It's remarkable how a wife who can spot a blond hair on her husband's coat clear across the room, can't see a pair of garage doors twelve feet wide.

You can tell a woman is married by the ring on her finger—but you can't tell her much.

A loving wife will do anything for her husband except stop criticizing him and trying to improve him. (*John B. Priestley*)

Puzzler: why a woman complains her husband doesn't love her if he isn't a big provider, and sure he doesn't if he works so hard providing for her that he's too pooped-out to make love to her.

Storm Warnings

At length he stretches out his foolish head to the conjugal bed. (*Juvenal*)

Needles and pins, needles and pins, when a man marries, his trouble begins. (*James Orchard Halliwell*)

We wedded men live in sorrow and care. (*Chaucer*)

A young man married is a man that's marr'd. . . . When I said I would die a bachelor, I did not think I would live till I were married. (*Shakespeare*)

Husbands vs. Wives

Ne'er take a wife till thou hast a house (and a fire) to put her in. (*Benjamin Franklin*)

He loves his bonds, who, when the first are broke,/Submits his neck into a second yoke. (*Robert Herrick*)

Women are all alike. When they're maids, they're mild as milk; once make 'em wives, and they lean their backs against their marriage certificates, and defy you. (*Douglas Jerrold*)

In buying horses and in taking a wife, shut your eyes tight and commend yourself to God. (*Tuscan proverb*)

When a man takes a wife, he ceases to dread Hell. (*Rumanian proverb*)

Every woman should marry—and no man. (*Benjamin Disraeli*)

A man is shorn of his strength if he belongs to one woman. (*Samuel Butler*)

She has buried all her female friends; I wish she would make friends with my wife. (*Martial*)

I wish Adam had died with all his ribs in his body. (*Boucicault*)

Since all the maids are good and lovable, from whence come the bad wives? (*Charles Lamb*)

Every man plays the fool once in his life, but to marry is playing the fool all one's life long. (*William Congreve*)

It is a woman's business to get married as soon as possible, and a man's to keep unmarried as long as he can. (*George Bernard Shaw*)

A man finds himself seven years older the day after his marriage. (*Francis Bacon*)

The Widows They Leave Behind

What is the world to a man whose wife is a widow? (*Irish proverb*)

The determination of life insurance salesmen to succed has made life pretty soft for widows. (*William Feather*)

Widows are dangerous animals to be at large. (*J. W. Stowe*)

The comfortable estate of widowhood is the only hope that keeps a wife's spirit up. (*John Gay*)

I have been to a funeral; I can't describe to you the howl which the widow set up at proper intervals. (*Charles Lamb*)

Widowhood is the financial remains of a love affair. (*George Jean Nathan*)

A buxom widow must either be married, buried, or shut up in a convent. (*Spanish proverb*)

Widows, like ripe fruit, drop easily from their perch. (*Jean de La Bruyère*)

My idea of walking into the jaws of death is marrying some woman who's lost three husbands. (*Kin Hubbard*)

The rich widow cries with one eye and rejoices with the other. (*Miguel de Cervantes*)

It's not always the brunet-dyed widows who remarry soonest; the light-headed ones don't do so badly either.

Husbands vs. Wives

These widows, sir, are the most perverse creatures in the world. (*Joseph Addison*)

Be very careful o' vidders all your life. (*Charles Dickens*)

The rich widow's tears soon dry. (*Danish proverb*)

A widow and her money are soon courted. (*Modern proverb*)

4
WIVES vs. HUSBANDS

Definitions

A *wife is* . . .

The proof that women can take a joke.

One for whom married life is one dish-appointment after another.

The power behind the drone.

A person who wouldn't try so hard to conceal her age if her husband acted his.

A woman who knows that the oyster is not the only one who has a crab for a mate.

One whose mate takes his troubles like a man—he blames them all on her.

Wives vs. Husbands

A person who is expected to sit up with her husband when he is sick, and put up with him when he is not.

One who thought she was marrying a man in shining armor, and now finds herself shining pots and pans.

A woman who never ceases to wonder why a husband can't show as much patience at home as when he's waiting for a fish to bite.

One who vowed when she married that it was for keeps; and it is. She keeps on working and keeps house.

A person who can look in the top drawer of a dresser and find a man's handkerchief and socks that aren't there.

One who likes the simple things of life—which explains why she married the man she did.

A woman who is expected to be a sweetheart, a nurse, a cook, a laundress, a seamstress, and an audience.

A person who is no longer hoping—just expecting.

A woman with a mate who hires someone to mow his lawn so he can play golf for exercise.

A woman with a mate from whom she has to take a lot for grunted.

A female spouse so indestructible, so delectable, and so deductible.

A married woman who is expected to look as sprightly as a girl, behave at all times like a well-mannered lady, think like a man, and work like a dog.

One whose husband married her to escape from lots of other women, and then chase other women to forget he's married to her.

A person who can't understand how a husband can spend any money during the day when he doesn't go to a beauty shop or the supermarket.

One whose husband admires her for her brains—brains enough to tell him how wonderful he is.

A woman who at times doesn't treat her husband as she should—and he ought to be thankful for it.

One whose husband expects her to be perfect, and to understand why he isn't.

A conceited husband's halter ego.

A clever creature whose husband thinks he's smarter than she is.

A person who handles her man like a toothpaste tube—she gives him a squeeze to get something out of him.

A woman who has learned how not to get up with a grouch —she gets up before him.

One who constantly wonders how a husband, who knows so much about economics, finance, and money, has so little of it.

The most efficient lie detector without wires.

One who can never understand why a man will show his worst side to his better half.

An overburdened housewife who often thinks she wouldn't mind being replaced by automation.

One who didn't want to be an old maid and look for a husband every day, and now looks for him every night.

Wives vs. Husbands

One whose husband can look at her without seeing her, whereas she can see right through him without even looking at him.

A man's best home remedy.

One whose husband brings home the bacon, but forgets the applesauce.

Familiar Types

DISILLUSIONED WIFE

One whose man was her ideal before marriage, and is now an ordeal.

A woman who married a man because he was a dreamer, and now finds him just a sleeper.

A female whose husband is living by the sweat of his frau.

One who wishes she had known her husband when he was alive.

One who thought before they were married that her man was worth his weight in gold, but he just hasn't panned out.

A woman who before marriage used to close her eyes when her husband kissed her; now she's sorry she didn't close his.

One who searched for a smart cookie, and wound up with a crumb.

HAPPY WIFE

A woman who is so much in love with her husband that every morning before he leaves for the office, she gift-wraps his lunch.

One who is able to count the men in her life on the third finger of her left hand.

MODERN WIFE

One who holds down a job outside the home to get a little leisure time.

OPTIMISTIC WIFE

One who married a man to reform him, thinking that the rites would right him, and the altar would alter him.

PREGNANT WIFE

A woman who wishes that her husband could bear with her.

SMART WIFE

A woman who knows that the best way to get around her husband is with her arms.

One who has the steaks on when her husband returns from a fishing trip.

A discerning female who realizes that if she wears the pants in the family, some other woman may be wearing the minks.

One who may not have gotten the best husband, but is making the best of the one she has.

A woman who laughs at all her husband's jokes, not because they're always clever, but because she is.

One who retains her girlish figure to keep up with her boyish husband.

A married woman who plays bridge, golf, tennis, and dumb.

A female who is not only interested in being logical, but zoological.

Wives vs. Husbands

One who makes sure that her husband can't afford another woman.

TRUTHFUL WIFE

A married woman who doesn't lie about anything except her age, her weight, and her husband's salary.

Husbands (of a Sort)

ABSENTMINDED HUSBAND

One who complains to his wife that his secretary doesn't understand him.

A chap who has his mail sent to the golf course, and plays all day with his secretary.

CONCEITED HUSBAND

A man who claims he never made a mistake, but has a wife who did.

CONSIDERATE HUSBAND

One who can be counted on to carry the stool when there's a piano to be moved.

A man who is always willing to buy his wife a new summer outfit—a package of seeds and a rake.

A man who hates to see his wife bent over a hot stove, so he buys her a higher stove.

One who regularly takes his wife window-wishing.

One who when his wife drops something kicks it over to where she can pick it up easier.

A fellow who steadies the stepladder for his wife while she paints the kitchen ceiling.

EGOTISTICAL HUSBAND

A man who, if he had to live his life over again, would still fall in love with himself.

FAITHFUL HUSBAND

A wolf who has grown tired.

FAITHLESS HUSBAND

A man who considers himself too good to be true.

One whose timing is perfect; so is his two-timing.

A mate who has circles under his eyes from keeping a triangle under his hat.

One who has a wife to appeal to his finer side and loftier instincts, and a woman on the side to help him forget them.

A man who doesn't mind his wife keeping her beauty secrets so long as he can keep his beauties secret.

One who suffers from high blonde pressure.

INDIFFERENT HUSBAND

One whose thoughts have turned from passion to pension.

JEALOUS HUSBAND

A man who is not sure of his wife because he is not sure of himself.

MEAN HUSBAND

One who shuts off his hearing aid when his wife offers her side of the argument.

A mate who is suffering from a hardening of the hearteries.

Wives vs. Husbands

MISUNDERSTOOD HUSBAND
One whose wife really understands him.

MODEL HUSBAND
One no woman should marry. According to the dictionary, a "model" is "a small imitation of the real thing."

A man who treats his wife as if she were his mistress.

MODERN HUSBAND
A person whose idea of exercise is to be out seven nights running.

One who is supporting his wife in the maner to which she is accustomed; he lets her keep her job.

OVERWEIGHT HUSBAND
A married man who should consider mending his weighs.

One whom a woman married because he was spic and span, but who now has more span than spic.

A mate whose only exercise is moving food from the plate to the palate.

One whose wife can't help having fun at his expense.

A paunchy fellow, whose wife would like him better if she could see him less.

SMART HUSBAND
One who if he should forget his wife's birthday would say, "Dear, how did you expect me to remember it when you don't look a day older?"

SOLICITOUS HUSBAND
A person who is so interested in his wife's happiness, he hires a detective to find out who's responsible for it.

STINGY HUSBAND

An economaniac.

A man whose wife wants pearls for her birthday, so he gives her an oyster and a rabbit's foot.

One whose doctor tells him his wife needs sea air, so he fans her with a mackerel.

A fellow who if his wife wants a fur coat gets her a trap and a gun.

One who when his wife asks for clothes money tells her to "go to the best shops and pick some nice things—but don't get caught."

One who is suffering from costrophobia.

A man who takes his wife window-wishing.

A fellow to whom money means nothing at all. When his wife asks for money, she gets nothing.

One who likes his wife in clinging dresses—the ones that have been clinging to her for years.

A person whose only interest in his wife's clothes is what they cost.

SUCCESSFUL HUSBAND

One who owes his prosperity to *push*—his wife's.

TACTLESS HUSBAND

An indiscreet mate, as in the case of the man who wrote his wife from Rome: "I have been visting the ruins, and thinking of you."

Wives vs. Husbands

THOUGHTFUL HUSBAND

One who leaves the lawn mower where his wife can easily find it.

WEAKLING HUSBAND

A married man who can always beer up under misfortune and when things aren't going his way.

The Wife's Marry-Go-Round

When a man makes a woman his wife, it is the highest compliment he can make her, and it's usually the last. (*Helen Rowland*)

A married woman soon learns that husbands are of three kinds: prizes, surprises, and consolation prizes.

A smart woman can manage a smart man, but it takes a brilliant woman to manage a bullheaded husband.

Women who marry men to mend their ways often find they aren't worth a darn.

A woman loves a husband who is a real lamb—provided he isn't growing sheepish with age.

Try praising your wife, even if it does frighten her at first. (*Billy Sunday*)

"Adam knew his wife and she conceived." It is a pity that this is still the only knowledge of their wives at which some men seem to arrive. (*Francis Herbert Bradley*)

A woman isn't as interested in making a man over as merely trying to get him to be what he claimed to be before they were married.

The only time most husbands can keep their wives guessing is when they're dancing with them.

Many a wife would cheerfully exchange her wedding presents for a good lie detector.

A husband who complains he's henpecked might try increasing his wife's chicken-feed allowances.

For some women, marriage is like a phone call at 2:00 A.M. She gets a ring, and then wakes up.

The one big trouble with lovemaking in marriage is that wives would like their husbands to put a little more love into it.

A husband who is as busy as a bee may wake up one day to find his honey missing.

The silliest woman can manage a clever man, but it needs a very clever woman to manage a fool. (*Rudyard Kipling*)

A married woman is as old as her husband makes her feel. (*Arthur Wing Pinero*)

The man who criticizes his wife's taste is apt to overlook the fact that she picked him for a husband.

The chief reason why wives don't go on strike is that there are too many strikebreakers.

Every man who is high up loves to think that he has done it all himself, and the wife smiles, and lets it go at that. (*James M. Barrie*)

Before marriage, a man will lie awake all night thinking about something you said; after marriage, he'll fall asleep before you finish saying it. (*Helen Rowland*)

Wives vs. Husbands

When they first meet, a man will tell a woman about his throbbing heart; after marriage all he talks about is his liver.

A man likes his wife to be just clever enough to comprehend his cleverness, and just stupid enough to admire it. (*Israel Zangwill*)

The trouble with most wives is their trouble with their husbands.

A husband who expects his wife to sing his song had better be sure that he's not off-key.

A wife is justified in not speaking to her husband for quite a time—for quite a time he had with another woman.

Many a married woman regrets that she didn't keep the bouquet at the wedding and throw the groom away.

If a woman is wearing her wedding ring on the wrong finger, it may be her way of saying that she's married to the wrong man.

Think what cowards men would be if they had to bear children. Woman are altogether a superior species. (*George Bernard Shaw*)

There are some husbands who never chase other women; they're too fine, too decent—but mostly too old.

The experienced wife knows that the best way to keep a husband is—in doubt.

A sure way of getting an erring husband back from an extended vacation is to send him the local paper with an item cut out of it.

One of a mother's hardest tasks is to convince her daughter that there are fine men in the world who are not exactly like Dad.

For every man there's a woman—and it's lucky for a husband if his wife doesn't know about her.

Many a wife who tries to get her husband to learn those new dances soon realizes she can't teach his old dogs new tricks.

The only remedy if a man won't give his wife a divorce is to have ten children by him; that way, she can lose him in a crowd.

It's a shrewd girl who isn't as interested in marrying a go-getter as an already got-'er.

A woman needs only three words to insure marital happiness: "My, you're wonderful!"

The happiest wives are those whose husbands love them a lot and do not try to understand them.

When you see what some girls marry, you realize how they must hate to work for a living. (*Helen Rowland*)

If wives only knew what secretaries think of their husbands, they'd stop worrying.

Wives know that if God made them without a sense of humor, it was so they could love their husbands instead of laughing at them.

What a pity it is that nobody knows how to manage a wife but a bachelor. (*George Colman*)

The man who thinks he's smarter than his wife is married to a smart woman.

Wives vs. Husbands

Many a woman married a man thinking he'd be a real comforter, only to find him just a wet blanket.

The road to success is filled with women pushing their husbands along. (*Thomas Dewar*)

With some women it's harder to find a husband after marriage than before.

The best husband a woman can have is an archaeologist; the older she gets, the more he is interested in her.

Many a wife's head on her husband's shoulder accomplishes more than his does.

The husband who opens the door and assists his wife into the car has very likely just acquired one or the other.

A woman, if she has the misfortune of knowing anything, should conceal it as well as she can. (*Jane Austen*)

There are two kinds of husbands: those who bring their wives a gift on their return from a trip, and those who behaved themselves.

A woman can always tell when her husband is pulling the wool over her eyes by the sheepish grin on his face.

Men are but children, too, though they have gray hairs; they are only of a larger size. (*Seneca*)

Pity the woman who regarded marriage as a union of two souls, only to find herself hitched to a heel.

Wives agree that one of the advantages of being a man is that you don't have to kiss someone who hasn't shaved for a couple of days.

Some wives simply cannot find words to describe their feelings about their husbands—they're much too ladylike to use them.

Perhaps some women watch those sobby TV soap-opera programs so that their own marriages won't seem so sad.

When a man brings flowers home to his wife for no reason, it's a safe bet that there's a reason.

'Tis strange what a man may do, and a woman yet think him an angel. (*William Makepeace Thackeray*)

The smart wife knows that only one woman in the whole world can have the best husband, so she makes the best of the one she has.

The allowance some husbands give can't compare with the allowances their wives make.

A fortune awaits someone who can invent transparent paper for newspapers, so that wives can see their husbands at the breakfast table.

Often the man who admits he's married to "the right woman," could go a step further and admit she has brains enough for two.

It's as hard to get a man to stay home after you've married him as it was to get him to go home before you married him. (*Helen Rowland*)

A good husband makes a good wife. (*Robert Burton*)

Chief among the things that husbands don't understand about their wives is how their wives understand so much about them.

A man needs two women in his life—a secretary to take everything down and a wife to pick everything up.

One sure way that a woman has of finding out what kind of a husband she doesn't want is to marry him.

Wives vs. Husbands

The man who says that his wife made a fool of him might stop and think that maybe she merely gave him an opportunity to develop his natural capacities.

Maybe the reason some woman are always knitting is because if they didn't do something with their hands they'd choke their husbands.

The way some husbands throw their clothes around, they must be suffering from clothesthrowphobia.

Widows are not the only women who have late husbands.

Nothing makes a man's little knowledge so dangerous as thinking his wife doesn't have it.

Storm Warnings

Women when they marry buy a cat in the bag. (*Montaigne*)

But marriage is a fetter and a snare,/A hell, no lady so polite can bear. (*George W. Young*)

Marriage is a lottery; every wife does not become a widow. (*Israel Zangwill*)

If it is true that girls are inclined to marry men like their fathers, it is understandable why mothers cry at weddings. (*Anonymous*)

A wife is a receptacle of half a man's cares, and two-thirds of his ill-humor. (*Charles Reade*)

Being a woman is a terribly difficult trade, since it consists principally of dealing with men. (*Joseph Conrad*)

Some ladies are too beauteous to wed,/For where's there a man that's worthy of their bed? (*Young*)

Women have been so highly educated, that nothing should surprise them except a happy marriage. (*Oscar Wilde*)

It takes a man twenty-five years to learn to be married; it's a wonder women have the patience to wait for it. (*Clarence Buddington Kelland*)

Intelligent women always marry fools. (*Anatole France*)

The majority of husbands remind me of an orang-outang trying to play the violin. (*Balzac*)

There is nothing in the world like the devotion of a married woman. It is something no married man knows anything about. (*Oscar Wilde*)

A man marries one woman to escape from many others, and then chases many others to forget he's married to one. (*Helen Rowland*)

Definitions

A legal formula that follows "I do" with "Adieu."

The result of holy wedlock turned into an unholy deadlock.

The transition from coo-existence to go-existence.

Hash made from domestic scraps.

What happens when the transposition of the letter *I* has turned marital relationship into a martial one.

The result of compatibility turning into combatibility.

The banked fires of the flame of love.

The refuge of a man and woman who find they weren't fit to be tied.

A popular pastime for couples who were mispronounced man and wife.

The proof that one man's mate is another man's poison.

A case of marriage giving out because there wasn't enough giving in.

A legal device for people who believe "United we stand, but divided we can stand it better."

The result of a transition from a duet to a duel.

The legal recourse of a husband who files suit because of an extra pair of pants.

The final step in a dreamy waltz in ¾ time where one of the parties started to two-time.

A separation, in the land of the free and the home of the brave, by a couple who would rather be free than brave.

A legal dissolution of a marriage where the trouble with the wedlock was not enough wed and too much lock.

A legal device for couples who believe their marriage vow was "to love and cherish, till the death of love do us part."

The marital grave made by couples with a series of little digs.

A case of lovers becoming leavers.

When a marriage tie becomes a forget-me-knot.

A severance of the ties that blind.

The aspirin tablet for marital headaches.

Divorce

A legal recourse for a couple who are determined to prove that love can find a way—out.

A judicial solution for injudicious people.

The storm in the port of a couple who started out with the thought of a port in the storm.

Matrimony's Great Divide.

The proof that truce is stranger than fiction.

The proof that there are cowards who won't fight to a finish.

For some people, the result of boredom, because it combines for them the minimum of temptation with the maximum of opportunity.

What happens when couples stop toasting and start roasting each other.

The result of unpleasant relations—such as in-laws, uncles, aunts, et cetera.

The past tense of a tense marriage.

The finale of a drama in three acts: Announced, Denounced, Renounced.

The decree obtained by a woman whose husband's sole interest was in gals and gallons.

The decree obtained by a woman whose husband suffers from a chronic ailment—high blonde pressure.

The decree obtained by a woman whose husband was so busy earning his salt that he forgot his sugar.

The decree obtained by a husband because his wife threw his coat out—and he happened to be in it at the time.

The decree obtained by a husband because his wife began to feel like a new man.

The proof that some couples nowadays marry for love, some for a home, but most for a short time.

A legal dissolution for couples who believe in enduring love —if it doesn't have to be endured too long.

A popular pastime which put alimony into matrimony.

DIVORCE COCKTAIL

Marriage on the Rocks.

DIVORCE COURT

Next to doctors, a convenient place to go to for a headache.

Where people who vowed to be tried and true are often tried because they were untrue.

DIVORCED HUSBAND

The lover who courted a woman, the human being she married, and the brute she divorced.

DIVORCEE

A divorced female who is looking for fresh he-quipment.

One who, far from forgetting men, is for getting one as soon as possible.

One who has gotten richer by decrees.

DIVORCE EVIL

Alimony.

DIVORCE LAWYER

One who is paid hundreds of dollars to untie a knot that a clergyman was begrudged a few dollars for tying.

Divorce

DIVORCE SUIT

A legal proceeding for the dissolution of a marriage, called a suit because it is pressed with the seamy side out.

Adieu

Divorces are made in heaven. (*Oscar Wilde*)

There would be fewer divorces for such inconsequential reasons if people didn't get married for such inconsequential reasons.

Divorce dates from just about the same time as marriage; I think that marriage is a few weeks the more ancient. (*Voltaire*)

It's possible that it's called "grounds for divorce" because of the dirt.

A great number of divorces are due to the fact that the couples have nothing in common—nothing even to quarrel about.

Not the least among optimists are people who think that the persons they are about to marry are better than the ones they just divorced.

A lot of women are getting alimony who don't earn it. (*Don Herold*)

Paper napkins never return from a laundry, nor love from a trip to the law courts. (*John Barrymore*)

One of the reasons for so many divorces is that too many girls get married before they can adequately support a husband.

An Irreverent Dictionary of Love and Marriage

The only time some couples are seen together after their wedding is in the divorce court.

There are undoubtedly some old-fashioned wives—ones who have not been divorced more than twice.

It would seem, with divorces so easy to obtain nowadays, that the only prerequisite for a divorce is a marriage license.

If married people went everywhere their mates told them, there would be fewer divorces but more widows and widowers.

Lots of married people get divorced because of poor eyesight—they can't see each other from a hole in the wall.

If divorces didn't separate constantly quarreling couples, the police would have to do so.

Most divorces result, not from aversion or hostility, but from indifference.

Judging by the large number of divorces, it is apparent that what is sorely needed is a stronger lock in wedlock.

There would be many more divorces if it weren't for the disinclination on the part of a husband or a wife to make the *other happy*!

Viewing the great number of divorces sought by women, one wonders whether the modern woman wants a man for a hubby or a hobby.

Many a wife sues for divorce because of a miss-understanding.

It is often the little things that break up a marriage—little blondes, little brunettes, little redheads.

Divorce

Many wives have solved the problem of how to get rid of their old dishwashers. They divorce them.

The real reason why so many men are prompt with their alimony payments is their fear of being repossessed by their ex-wives if they miss a single one.

The three most beautiful words in the English language to a divorced woman are "Alimony check enclosed."

Many a divorce-seeking husband would have been more interested in the woman in his life if there had been more life in his woman.

Juries nowadays are quick to grant a divorce after reading a mate's diary from lover to lover.

Lots of wives are granted divorces because of their husbands' knee trouble—like finding a blonde on it.

Maybe the modern woman doesn't marry a man for his money, but she certainly seems to be divorcing him for it.

It used to be that folks consulted a masseur to get rid of a pain in the neck. Now they get a divorce.

Formerly, people went to a doctor for something to quiet their nerves. Now they go to a lawyer—for a divorce.

It's not surprising that so many women go back to live with their ex-husbands, considering what they had to go through to collect their alimony checks.

Many a wife seeking a divorce isn't doing so because there's any other man in her life. It's just that she's determined there will be.

If they had to do it over again, numerous divorced couples would still marry each other—at the point of a gun.

No man is fully aware of his high cash-surrender value until he's sued for divorce and alimony.

Perhaps the best definition of incompatibility is where one of the parties wants a divorce, and the other doesn't.

Statistics show that one out of four married couples get divorced—the other three just fight it out to the bitter end.

ODDS AND ENDS

Behind every successful man stands a devoted wife--and a surprised mother-in-law.

The very thought of marriage unnerves a lot of bachelors. Of course it unnerves a lot of husbands too.

Men are no longer marrying women on $75 a week—a girl must be earning much more than that.

Confessions by husbands and wives may be good for the soul, but they're bad for harmony and peace.

There's one thing that can be said for marriage as a wonderful institution. Without it, husbands and wives would have to fight with strangers.

Some married people who complain that they don't get all they deserve should congratulate themselves.

It's more than likely that when Eve approached Adam for the first time in the Garden of Eden, she inquired, "Have you been waiting long?"

The fellow who's ready to give you the shirt off his back undoubtedly got it from his wife or children on Father's Day.

According to statistics, an astonishing percentage of men try to avoid married life; this includes those who are married, too.

When a man tells his wife that her new hat looks good on her, he probably hasn't seen the price tag.

Some women not only meet their husbands half way, but even go the whole way—right to the office on pay day.

The views expressed by some husbands in their homes are not necessarily those of the management.

It's unfair for a newly wedded woman to require her husband to pay for the clothes contracted before marriage—it's like asking a fish to pay for the bait he was caught with.

It is not exactly factual that some first children come too early—it's just that some weddings come too late.

Girls who make love from A to Z often look like H—.

A man's voice that is most pleasing to a girl is one that has an engagement ring in it.

The best oral contraceptive for an unmarried girl is still No.

Girls who start out playing with fire, usually end up cooking over it.

Odds and Ends

Youth calls to youth—and it's no wonder that the telephone company keeps prospering.

The only difference in the game of love since primordial times is that trumps have been changed from clubs to diamonds.

Where a successful wooing once depended largely on what a fellow sent a girl, it depends nowadays on how.

If that silly giggle sounds like a rippling brook—young man, you're in love!

They say that a modest girl doesn't run after a man. Naturally! Does a mousetrap run after a mouse?

Girls who insist "I never did anything like this before" must have inherited a lot of experience.

Finding a needle in the proverbial haystack is often easier than finding it in a modern girl's hand.

Telling some modern brides what they should know about marriage is like giving a fish a bath.

The best way for a girl to learn what men like is not by asking father what he thinks, but by asking mother what she knows.

The popular girl has studied all the angles on how to attract men, but a few curves are a big help too.

Flattery is the art of pretending you like the girl more than the kiss.

The trouble with being a bachelor is that by the time you've played the field you're too old to make a pitch.

This would be a far better world if there were more mistletoe and less missile talk.

A man who thinks he's smarter than his wife is married to a smart woman.

It often takes just one of a husband's kisses to arouse his wife—the one he gives some other woman at a party.

The woman who fishes for a husband had better make sure that she doesn't get one—hook, line, and stinker.

The biggest mystery to a wife is how a husband who bowls until 2 A.M. without making a strike, can manage to knock over all the milk bottles in the hallway.

Not all women are too hasty in leaving a husband who loafs half the time. Half a loafer is better than none.

Any woman can get her husband to do some of the harder work around the house by hinting that he's probably getting too old for it.

In some oriental countries, a man never takes a girl out until after marriage. American wives prefer a set-up like this to the one in this country where their husbands never take them out afterwards.

It may be dangerous for a woman to tell her husband that she loves him more than any other man in the world. He may suspect that she's been experimenting.

The married woman who once said she wouldn't marry the best man in the world is now ready to confide that she didn't.

When a woman claims she's married to a gentleman and a scholar, it could be that she's a bigamist.

The woman who marries a widower can cure him of talking about his first wife by starting to talk about her next husband.

Odds and Ends

The only time some wives hear a laugh around the house is when their husbands are reading the comics.

Many a chap who boasted that he was a do-it-yourself man was lucky to get a get-it-done wife.

The smart wife treats her husband in such a way that it would take more than an electric blanket to replace him.

The husband who gets all puffed up when his wife says he's one in a million may not realize that she means he's the wrong one.

A man may ask his wife for the right to take out his blonde secretary, and she may let him have it. When he gets up, she'll let him have it again.

The shrewd wife examines the matchbooks in her husband's pockets. It's lots cheaper than hiring a detective.

To the man's question, "Whatever became of the old-fashioned woman who fainted when a man kissed her?" the woman's comeback is: "Whatever happened to the old-fashioned men who made them faint?"

When a man asks a women to share his lot, she might do well to ask him to show her the size of it.

The playboy husband whose unsuspecting wife thinks he's the eighth wonder of the world will really be in trouble if she catches him fooling around with the other seven.

The sure cure for a wife's inferiority complex is to be ill for a few days while her husband manages the house and the children.

Ask any wife for the definition of a good husband, and she'll answer: "A domesticated wolf."

Newspapers are filled with reports of wives shooting their husbands. Women are apparently here to slay.

Any husband can tell you why King Solomon had 1,000 wives—so he could come home after a hard day's work and find at least one in good humor.

Don't think that every disconsolate man has loved and lost —he may have won her.

Many a wife takes an active interest in her husband's work —opening his pay envelope, for instance.

The man who is admired by his wife's relatives can truly face all the rest of the world dauntlessly.

The man who as a bachelor yearns for the peace, quiet, and comfort of married life may find after marriage that he still does.

There's a reason why some men choose plump wives: They'd rather live with 150 pounds of curves than 100 pounds of nerves.

Husbands agree that wives don't cry so much anymore, but then, what has she to cry about?

Put down as a snide official report the one published in a local newspaper: "Police can find no reason for suicide. The man was unmarried."

It's a heroic husband indeed who is brave enough to phone his wife's bridge club to say that it's time to break up the game so she can go home to get supper.

Many a man doesn't really start living until he's married— then he's finished.

Odds and Ends

A husband doesn't always lie to his wife. Some nights the little woman is too tired to ask questions.

There is no better way to remember your wife's birthday than to forget it just once.

Who says that there can be no meeting of minds in marriage? Of course, it's the wife who usually presides.

Any husband can tell you where the Holywood and TV producers get their ideas for horror movies. It's from seeing their wives with their hair up in curlers and their faces smeared with cold cream.

The reason marriage hasn't brought music into some husbands' lives is that they haven't learned to play second fiddle.

A recent poll shows that a considerable number of husbands have stopped helping their wives with the dishes— they're doing them all by themselves now.

The average husband knows he has the legal right to open his wife's mail—all he needs now is the courage.

It cannot be denied that many a wife has helped her husband to the top of the ladder; but it would be even nicer if she didn't then decide that the picture would look better on another wall.

A good way to stop the noise in your car is to leave your wife at home.

The shrew who complains that her husband always called her "sweetheart" before they were married, and now doesn't call her anything, should be grateful for his self-restraint.

One way a husband might cure his wife of nervousness is to tell her it's a symptom of advancing age.

Many a husband who takes a trip to Rome can't do as the Romans do—he has his wife with him.

It's a persuasive husband who can convince his wife, if she catches him with his secretary on his knee, that because business is so bad he's learning to be a ventriloquist.

A fortune awaits some entrepreneur who will start a school that will teach husbands to pack suitcases so that they can leave home.

An optimist has been defined as a single man contemplating marriage. There are husbands who would be inclined to define a pessimist as a married man contemplating marriage.

Many a husband remembers when he proposed—it was when she stopped twisting his arm.

Advice to a husband: Think twice before you speak—especially if you intend to say to your wife what you think.

Married men have been known to drive their wives crazy by just chuckling in their sleep, with a smug smile on their faces.

The man who says, "My wife is the most wonderful woman in the world," often confides in a whisper, "and that's not just my opinion—it's *Hers*."

A wife will stay with a husband who has a will of his own—especially if it's made out to her.

A husband's conception of "creeping inflation" is when his wife starts out to buy a new hat, and winds up with a complete new outfit.

It's a dumb husband who doesn't get the point when his wife starts wrapping his lunch in a road map.

Odds and Ends

Statistics show that 70 per cent of the wives who got new mink coats did so "After the Bawl Was Over."

The average husband's monthly salary runs into three figures—his wife and two daughters.

Some wives have simple tastes. They enjoy nothing more than having their husbands read to them—from a bankbook.

An extravagant woman's husband has good cause to worry about her rapidly expanding wasteline.

A husband and wife each have their share of worries. He worries about what the future has in store for him, and she worries about what the stores have in the future.

High up among the reasons why husbands leave home are wives who can cook but don't, and wives who can't cook but do.

Many men miss their wives' cooking—every chance they get.

Every unmarried man should study botany to learn the difference between a clinging vine and a power plant.

There are lots of married men who drink as much as they used to when they were single—but then they used to drink out of pleasure.

The husband who yearns to die with his boots on will get his wish—if he ever wears them into the living room on cleaning day.

When a girl tells her fellow that he's her knight, he'd better be sure that he won't be her knight-*errand*.

In the days of old, knights fought with battle-axes. Some married men are still doing it.

Many a husband wishes he'd remained a bachelor so he'd only have to fix one breakfast before going to work.

With so many yes-men in American homes, there are wags who believe it should be called the Land of Nod.

Not all wives have large vocabularies. Some are women of few words—but they keep them mighty busy.

TV-program-rating services have a phone problem with husbands. When they inquire: "Who are you listening to right now?" the invariable answer is: "My wife."

A wife is wrong when she complains to her husband that every time he looks at a sexy blonde he forgets he's married. That's when he's *reminded.*

The surest way to cure yourself of gambling is to get married on a bet.

It's impossible for a woman to be married to the same man for any length of time. After a few years he's not the same man.

Grandchildren don't make a man feel old; it's the knowledge that he's married to a grandmother.

Life has a way of evening things out. For every man who marries for money there's a woman who marries for alimony.

Probably the worst triangle of all is where husband and wife are both in love with *him.*

Somewhere there must be a couple who got married and lived happily even after.

It must have been the twin bed manufacturers who invented and promoted women's hair curlers.

Odds and Ends

Husbands or wives can be cured of snoring by helpful advice, kindness, and patient cooperation—and by stuffing a sock in their mouths.

A recent survey reveals that one tenth of all married people aren't.

Some women know how to get even with their ex-husbands—they remarry them.

Sound advice: Don't marry for money. You can borrow it cheaper.

The husband who goes out with a perfect 36 had better be sure his wife doesn't come in with a loaded .45.

Many a playboy boss's wife picks a secretary for him who's neither a blonde nor a redhead—he has a mustache and is bald.

Some married people could never qualify for membership in the High Fidelity Record Club—they're low on fidelity and high on frequency.

The man who claims that he sees eye to eye with his wife might truthfully add that she's corrected his vision.

A man may be justified in thinking that his mother-in-law has a low opinion of him if the towels she gives his wife and him as a gift are marked HERS and ITS.

When a bride brings her mother along to live with her and her husband it is known as a "package deal."

There are men who have been married for several years and don't have any children—they have strict mothers-in-law.

Asked to donate something to the Old Ladies' Home, some men cheerfully offer to donate their mothers-in-law.

Husbands and wives have many arguments, with the wife only winning half of them. Her mother wins the other half.

No man is envied more by some husbands than Adam, who lived in Paradise without a mother-in-law.

More than one man has tried to get his mother-in-law to go fishing with him—all ready with an extra hook, line, and sink'er.

What hurts a man more than anything else is buying his mother-in-law a set of dentures, and then having her laugh at him with his own teeth.

When a fellow offers to give his mother-in-law a Jaguar for her birthday, she'd better be sure it doesn't have four legs.

Strange as it may seem, a guy can get a long jail term for cementing better family relations—like sealing his mother-in-law up behind a brick wall.

7 EPITAPHS
for departed spouses

Here lies my wife; here let her lie!
Now she is at rest—and so am I.
—*by John Dryden*

SACRED TO THE MEMORY OF JARED BATES
His widow lives at 7 Elm Street, has every qualification of a good wife, and YEARNS to be comforted.
—*Lincoln, Maine*

REST IN PEACE, DEAR HUSBAND—UNTIL WE MEET AGAIN
Middlebury, Vermont

Here lies my wife, a sad slattern and shrew;
If I said I regretted her, I should lie too.
—*Selby, Yorkshire*

       IN MEMORY
     BETSY FITZHUGH
        My wife
        lies here.
        I am glad
        of it.
—*Brookfield, Connecticut*

Beneath these stones do lie,
Back to back, my wife and I!
When the last trumpet the air shall fill,
If she gets up, I'll just lie still.
—*Sargentville, Maine*

Here lies Pierre Cobachard, grocer.
His inconsolable widow dedicates this monument to his memory, and continues the same business at the old stand, 167 Rue Mouffertard.
—*Pere-la-Chaise Cemetery, Paris*

Here lies my wife in earthly mould,
Who when she lived did naught but scold.
Peace! wake her not, for now she's still.
She had; but now I have my will.
—*Bayfield, Mississippi*

Epitaphs for Departed Spouses

Here I lie between my two wives.
But I have requested my relatives to
tip me a little toward Tillie.
—*Ontario*

Here lies my husbands, One, Two, Three
Dumb as men could ever be.
As for my Fourth, well praise be God,
He bides for a little above the sod.
Alex, Ben, Sandy were the first three's names,
And to make things tidy, I'll add his—James.
—*Shutesbury, Massachusetts*

Beneath this stone, a lump of clay, lies Arabella Young,
Who on the 24th of May began to hold her tongue.
—*Linton, England*

Stranger, call this spot not a place
Of fear and gloom;
To me it is a pleasant spot—
It is my husband's tomb.
—*Old English epitaph*

My grief is more than I can bear—ALONE.
—*Montgomery, Alabama*

> This stone was raised by Sarah's lord,
> Not Sarah's virtues to record—
> For they're well-known to all the town—
> But it was *raised* to keep her *down*.
> —Kilmurry Churchyard, Ireland

Some other wry, droll and pointed headstone inscriptions discovered in churchyards throughout the world, and worthy here of note, are:

> Maria Brown, Wife of Timothy Brown
> She lived with her husband 50 years, and died in the confident hope of a better life.

> Here lies my husband, Augustus Brauder, who was accidentally killed in his 58th year. This monument is erected by his grateful wife.

> My husband lies here;
> All my tears cannot bring him back.
> Therefore I weep.

> Here lies a woman who was always tired;
> She lived in a house where help was not hired;
> Her last words were, "Dear friends, I am going
> Where washing ain't done, nor sweeping nor sewing;
> Don't mourn for me now, don't mourn for me never,
> I'm going to do nothing, forever and ever.

Epitaphs for Departed Spouses

No references to epitaphs for departed spouses could be complete without the inclusion of the grieving widow's inscription on her husband's tombstone: "The Light of My Life Has Gone Out." Not long after the gentleman's demise, she met and wed another man; whereup she requested the monument maker to modify the inscription, to read:

> The Light of My Life Has Gone Out.
> P.S. I Found a Match.